*There I Was at 20,000 Feet . . .*

# *There I Was at 20,000 Feet . . .*

## The Best of RAF Humour

Jack Spence

BLANDFORD

**Blandford**
An imprint of Cassell
Villiers House, 41/47 Strand, London WC2N 5JE



First published 1990
Reprinted 1990

Distributed in the United States by
Sterling Publishing Co. Inc.
387 Park Avenue South, New York, NY 10016–8810

Distributed in Australia by
Capricorn Link (Australia) Pty Ltd
PO Box 665, Lane Cove, NSW 2066

**British Library Cataloguing in Publication Data**

There I was at 20,000 feet: the best of RAF humour.
1. Humour in English, 1945–. Special subjects. Great Britain, Royal Air Force. Anthologies
I. Spence, Jack
827'.914'080356

ISBN 0–7137–2147–2

Typeset by Fakenham Photosetting Ltd, Fakenham, Norfolk

Printed and bound in Great Britain by
Mackays of Chatham PLC, Chatham, Kent

# Contents

# Foreword

I first encountered the RAF style of humour within seconds of passing through the main entrance at Padgate when I joined the Service in 1946. Shouts of 'you'll be sorry' came from the 'Janker Wallahs', who were being productively employed outside the Guardroom, whitewashing coal and arranging the lumps neatly in steel bins burnished like the breastplates of the Household Cavalry. I quickly realized that no matter how hard the going was, how miserable the surroundings or the circumstances were, there was always someone ready to make light of the situation and raise a smile with a joke or appropriate wisecrack.

Later on I was to appreciate the importance of humour in the exercise of leadership. This has long been the case, especially in the early days of flying, when cheating the Grim Reaper was a full-time occupation—that era produced such great warriors as 'Batchy' Atcherley and his twin brother, David, and the well-known Earl of Bandon (the abandoned Earl). These fun-loving yet outstanding pilots created more than their share of mayhem throughout their Service careers but at the same time were quite brilliant leaders who thoroughly and ostentatiously enjoyed every minute of every day.

But, of course, the humour exists at all levels and ranks, and long may it continue thus. After all, we shouldn't have joined if we couldn't take a joke.

Air Chief Marshal Sir Thomas Kennedy GCB AFC DL
Controller, Royal Air Force Benevolent Fund

# Introduction

The Royal Air Force was formed on All Fools Day, 1918, and its members have been laughing with one another ever since.

My research for this book soon confirmed my belief that individuals will quite naturally laugh in the face of adversity, ridicule pomposity and be amused by their own foolishness. These characteristics have never been better demonstrated than by those who have served over the years with the Royal Air Force. Whenever or wherever a group of airmen congregates (particularly if there is an adjacent bar), the sound of laughter inevitably resounds as flying stories are recounted, characters are remembered and amusing incidents are recalled.

It was therefore no surprise to me when my requests for humorous material received such an overwhelming response. I am extremely grateful to all those contributors and helpers who, through their efforts and generosity, have supported The Fund and provided me with much amusement and pleasure during the compilation of this book.

Wherever possible I have specified the place and date of the anecdotes that are known to be true, on most occasions using the rank of the narrator at the time of the incident. Other stories may have been invented, but, like all yarns, they are no doubt based to some extent on reality.

So, whether it is Pilot Officer Prune 'shooting a line', a spoof at the expense of an over-confident chum, Douglas Bader milking a threatening situation to the embarrassment of the 'Goons', an hilarious David Langdon wartime cartoon or simply some poor chap making a monkey of himself, I hope there are lots of items within these covers to amuse all those readers who have an affection for the 'Boys in Blue'.

Squadron Leader Jack Spence, RAF (Retired)

# Acknowledgements

*For permission to reproduce extracts from other publications:*

Punch Publications Limited
Reader's Digest Association Limited
Midas Books
Severn House Publishers Limited
Collins Publishers Limited
Harrap Limited
Merlin Books Limited
A. M. Heath & Company Limited
Ian Allan Limited
Peters, Fraser and Dunlop
Unwin Hyman Limited
Thorsons Publishing Group Limited
Goodall Publications Limited
Chatto & Windus Limited
Muller, Blond and White Limited
David Langdon
Kenneth Wolstenholme
The Estate of Anthony Armstrong
MoD CS (Rep S)
MoD PCB (Air)
Squadron Leader Jack Currie

*For advice and assistance during research:*

Royal Air Force Museum
Department of Aviation Records MoD
Adastral House Library

*For photographic, design and artwork assistance:*

Karen Rainbird
Brian James
Bill Rose
Wing Commander Nigel Williams
Wing Commander Al Turner

*And all others who contributed to and assisted with completion of this book.*

## Acknowledgements of Sources

BARTLEY, Squadron Leader ANTHONY, DFC, *From the Journals of a Fighter Pilot*, William Kimber & Co. Ltd, London, 1984

BICKERS, RICHARD TOWNSHEND, *Ginger Lacey, Fighter Pilot, Battle of Britain Top Scorer*, Robert Hale Ltd, London, 1962 Reissued Cassell, London, 1988

BRICKHILL, PAUL, *Reach for the Sky—Douglas Bader, His Life Story*, William Collins Sons & Co. Ltd, 1954
—*The Dam Busters*, Evans Brothers Limited, London, 1951

CURRIE, JACK, *Lancaster Target, The Story of a Crew Who Flew from Wickenby*, New English Library, London, 1977

EDWARDS, JIMMY, *Take It from Me*, T. Werner Laurie Ltd, 1 Doughty Street, London WC1, London, 1953

EMBRY, Air Chief Marshal Sir BASIL, KCB KBE DSO DFC AFC, *Mission Completed*, Methuen & Co. Ltd, 1957

FORRESTER, LARRY, *Fly for Your Life: The Story of R. R. Stanford Tuck DSO DFC*, Frederick Muller Ltd, London, 1956

HARTNELL-BEAVIS, J. *Final Flight*, Merlin Books, Braunton, Devon, 1985

HOOPER, BILL, *The Passing of Pilot Officer Prune*, Midas Books, Tunbridge Wells, Kent, 1975

JOHNSON, Air Vice Marshal JAMES E. ('JOHNNIE'), *Wing Leader*, Chatto & Windus, London, 1956

RAFF and ARMSTRONG, ANTHONY, *Nice Types*, Methuen & Co. Ltd, London

THOMAS, S. EVELYN (compiler), *RAF Parade*, John England Publications Ltd, 3 Homewood Road, St Albans

TRIPP, MILES, *The Eighth Passenger, A Documentary Account of a World War 2 Bomber Crew*, William Heinemann, 1969

VERITY, HUGH, *We Landed by Moonlight, Secret RAF Landings in France 1940–44,* Ian Allan, Shepperton, Surrey, 1978



The author and publisher thank all those who supplied material for the book. Every attempt was made to identify and credit sources. The author and publisher regret where this has not proved possible.

# Book Extracts

## Bolingbrokes

He received his DSO, and the previously awarded bar to his DFC, from the King in an investiture ceremony held at Bircham Newton, Norfolk, a big Coastal Command base, on the afternoon of January 28th, 1941.

It was a very impressive ceremony, with bands blaring and neat boxes of white-belted airmen on parade in front of the giant hangars. It had snowed the day before, and it was still bitterly cold, with low, gun-metal clouds, and little islands of hard-packed snow squeaking under the marchers' boots.

Throughout the ceremony three twin-engined Bolingbroke aircraft patrolled round and round the base at a few hundred feet, wings rocking in the turbulent air—keeping vigil just in case a lone Hun tried for a hit-and-run raid.

The King was accompanied by the Queen and the two young Princesses. As Tuck stepped forward he noticed that Margaret, seated on the platform behind her father, was intent on watching the circling Bolingbrokes.

'I am glad to see you again,' His Majesty said. He spoke very slowly and deliberately, as if mentally polishing each word before uttering it. He looked drawn and tired, but not in the least nervous: his handshake was firm and his smile confident. 'I expect you are having an easier time of it now, with this weather?'

'Yes, sir, things are a lot quieter.'

'Ah well, it will do you good to relax for a change. By the way, where was it that I decorated you before?'

'Hornchurch, sir.'

'Yes, I remember now.' He smiled suddenly and glanced at the sky. 'It was a rather better day than this.' Tuck smiled back, and the King presented him with his medals. 'Once again, my congratulations.'

'Thank you very much, sir.' As he took the regulation two paces backwards and saluted, out of the corner of his eye he saw the younger Princess still craning her neck to watch the planes patrolling above.

When the ceremony was over and the Royal visitors were about to get into their cars, ten-year-old Margaret suddenly tweaked Tuck's sleeve, pointed upwards and said: 'Tell me, what kind of aeroplanes are these?'

Everyone stopped and turned towards them.

'These are called Bolingbrokes, Your Royal Highness.'

She frowned and cocked her head to one side. 'Aren't they Blenheims?'

'Well—yes, as a matter of fact a Bolingbroke is just a Blenheim with a long nose built on.'

She beamed, triumphant, and yelped: 'I jolly well thought so. Pa-pa said they were *Hudsons*!'

His Majesty was the first to roar with laughter. Even Elizabeth momentarily forgot her earnest formality and, chuckling and shaking her head, took her little sister's hand and led her on to the cars.

*Fly for Your Life: The Story of R. R. Stanford Tuck* DSO, DFC
Larry Forrester

# VE Day, 1945

As VE Day approached, Group-Captain Howie sent for me. 'Jimmy,' he said, 'you must ground yourself for a couple of days and lay on the celebrations.'

He insisted that the officers' mess should be thrown open to all ranks and an orgy was witnessed that night that will never be repeated. All day long I exulted over the Tannoy, 'A party for all ranks in the officers' mess to-night at 7.30. Bring your own mugs!' Eight or nine of the largest possible barrels of beer were set up in the dining-room and the place was cleared for the influx.

At the height of the party we ran out of taps for the barrels, but the airmen broached them just the same, holding their mugs under the ever-

flowing cascade of bitter. Naturally, a lot of beer went on the floor, and by the end of the evening the dining-hall was a couple of inches deep in the stuff.

The Station Commander drove round the camp seated on the roof of his staff car, with Corporal Sid Sharr at the wheel. On each knee of the brave Group-Captain was poised a WAAF, each brandishing a bottle of whisky.

*Take It from Me*, Jimmy Edwards

## No 610 Squadron, RAF Coltishall, 1942

I met Roger Franklin, senior controller, president of the mess committee and member of the Auxiliary Air Force. Roger ran his mess exceedingly well, was fond of his Sunday lunch-parties and generally saw to it that his mess members lived better than they were supposed to in those austere days of 1942. After all, the local lobsters were excellent, and Norfolk had always been famed for its game, war or no war. But on this occasion Roger was disgruntled. He had pranged his staff car and it was badly damaged. He had been on the mat before the group captain, and according to King's Regulations and Air Council Instructions, had been invited to pay £5 towards the cost of the damage.

Soon afterwards the enemy bombers came over Norwich at night and there was a lot of trade for the Beaufighters. The group captain drove to his Spitfire so that he could take off with the next Beaufighter and test his theory [that a Spitfire could 'use' a Beaufighter's radar contact]. His Spitfire was parked near the control tower and he taxied out fast, for precious seconds had already been lost. There was a lot of noise when the propeller of his Spitfire sliced into the roof of a staff car.

The following morning the MT officer was optimistic. The two damaged cars were of the same make and year, and he felt sure that one serviceable vehicle could be produced from the two wrecks. The course of action was obvious. At lunch-time, station commander met senior controller.

'Morning, Roger. Have a drink,' cheerfully invited the group captain.

'Thank you, sir,' replied Roger, who always kept his ear close to the ground. 'A pink gin, and I think you owe me two pounds ten!'

*Wing Leader*, 'Johnnie' Johnson

## No 610 Squadron, RAF Westhampnett, 1943

It was almost two years since Douglas Bader had begun to lead the Tangmere Wing from this same airfield, and curiously enough another legless pilot now joined the squadron. Colin Hodgkinson lost both his legs after a crash when serving with the Fleet Air Arm, but by following Bader's example and showing the same indomitable spirit he flew operationally and soon proved to be a valuable and aggressive member of our small team. Soon after our arrival we gave a party in our quarters, Woodcote Farm, and invited perhaps sixty or seventy officers from the other squadrons and the station. After all the guests had departed, a few of us sat amongst the debris, chatting about the evening and drinking a last half pint of beer. Hodgkinson made his excuses and clumped across the stone flags of the hall and up the stairs. Suddenly there was a loud crash when the legless pilot stumbled against the banisters, and pilot and banisters fell to the flags ten feet below. We rushed into the hall to find our pilot lying on the floor. He sat up and rubbed his head. I said:

'That was a hell of a drop. Are you all right? What about your legs, Colin?'

'Oh, they're quite all right, sir,' he answered.

'Are you sure? Perhaps we'd better call the doc?' I suggested.

'No, thank you, sir. You see, I fell on my head!'

*Wing Leader*, 'Johnnie' Johnson

## France, 1944

Since its introduction to the Service in 1939, the versatile Spitfire had participated in many diverse rôles and had fought over a variety of battlegrounds. It had appeared as a fighter, a fighter-bomber and as a tactical reconnaissance and photographic reconnaissance aircraft. Now it fulfilled yet another rôle, perhaps not so vital as some of the tasks it had undertaken in the past, but to us of supreme importance. Back in England, some ingenious mind had modified the bomb racks slung under each wing so that a small barrel of beer could be carried instead of a 500-pound bomb. Daily, this modern version of the brewers' dray flew across the Channel and alighted at St Croix. The beer suffered no ill effects from its unorthodox journey and was more than welcome in our mess.

*Wing Leader*, 'Johnnie' Johnson

# The Station Commander

The Group Captain Commanding an RAF Station—who is irreverently known as the Station-master—has much in common with the king of a lonely South Sea island. That is to say, they are both liable at any moment to have a Big White Chief arrive suddenly out of the blue in either a Large Shining Ship or a Large Shining Car and, in the voice of one speaking with bags of authority, tell them to do this, and stop doing that, and what the hell goes on here, and in general throw considerable weight around.

But in the intervals between these rare visitations from the outside world the power of the king of the South Sea island—or of the Master of the Station—is paramount. Fearfully paramount. His word is law. He has the power of life or death—or of leave and duty. No one gainsays him—because there's no one who dares to gainsay him. In fact, anyone who starts any gainsaying stuff round either island or Station will pretty soon find there's no future in it.

The Station Commander's activities are multifarious. He has to deal with an enormous mail. He has to grapple with hundreds of forms—one of the penalties of living under a Bumphocracy. He is perpetually interviewing delinquents, visitants, aspirants, applicants, supplicants, recalcitrants and sycophants.

He is also concerned with preventing any likelihood of a Wave of Crime sweeping the Station by arguments which can vary from mere Admonishment up to Twenty-eight Days in the Glasshouse.

In short he generally eagle-eyes the whole place from dawn to dawn.

And in A. C. Plonk's private opinion, he gives him (Plonk) an old-fashioned look whenever their paths cross.

By way of relaxation, the Station Commander sometimes flies on operations with his pilots. He also has at his disposal a small private aircraft—generally a 'Maggie'. He does not, of course, fly on operations in his 'Maggie', particularly not at a heavy bomber Station. It wouldn't look good.

He uses his 'Maggie' mostly for flipping over to other Stations to tell their Station-masters over lunch how much more efficient, successful and better-run his Station is than theirs. Later on they flip over to him and he plays a Home fixture.

To see the Station Commander and his 'Maggie', by the way, being got ready for a personal flight is rather like watching the finishing touches being given to a Derby favourite. Or a film star being got ready to go on the set. Or a prima donna about to make her big entrance.

An interesting sidelight on a Station Commander is that he rarely sees anyone sitting down, because whenever he's around everyone stands up.

Under the Station Commander you will find on the Station every sort of Air Force Nice Type, each with a different sphere of activity. This activity may be either genuine; or symbolic; or merely illusory—just a sort of mirage due to the Station Commander's passing.

*Nice Types*, Raff and Anthony Armstrong

# Operations Room, No 5 Group HQ, 16/17 May 1943

At Grantham a long silence had followed the flak warning at Huls, and then Dunn's phone rang sharply, and in the dead silence they all heard the Morse crackling in the receiver. It was quite slow and Cochrane, bending near, could read it. 'Goner,' he said. 'From G George.' 'Goner' was the code word that meant Gibson had exploded his bomb in the right place.

'I'd hoped one bomb might do it,' Wallis said gloomily.

'It's probably weakened it,' Cochrane soothed him. Harris looked noncommittal. There was no more from 'G George', and they went on waiting. A long silence. Nothing came through when Hopgood crashed. The phone rang, 'Goner' from 'P Popsie'. Another dragging silence. 'Goner' from 'A Apple'. Wallis swears even today that there was half an hour between each signal, but the log shows only about five minutes. 'Goner' from 'J Johnny'. That was Maltby, and the aura of gloom settled deeper over Wallis.

A minute later the phone rang again and the Morse crackled so fast the others could not read it. Dunn printed it letter by letter on a signals pad and let out a cry, 'Nigger. It's Nigger. It's gone.'

Wallis threw his arms over his head and went dancing round the room. The austere face of Cochrane cracked into a grin, he grabbed one of Wallis's hands and started congratulating him. Harris, with the first grin on his face that Wallis had ever seen, grabbed the other hand and said:

'Wallis, I didn't believe a word you said about this damn bomb, but you could sell me a pink elephant now.'

He said, a little later when some of the excitement had died down: 'I must tell Portal immediately.' Sir Charles Portal, Chief of the RAF, was in Washington that night on a mission, actually at that moment dining with Roosevelt. Harris picked up the nearest phone and said, 'Get me the White House.'

The little WAAF on the switchboard knew nothing of the highly secret raid. Even at Grantham, Cochrane's security had been perfect. She did not realize the importance of it all, or the identity of the great man who was speaking, and was caught off guard. 'Yes, sir,' she said automatically and, so they say, dialled the only White House she knew, a jolly little roadhouse a few miles out of Grantham.

Harris must have thought she was a very smart operator when the White House answered so quickly, and there are reported to have been moments of incredible and indescribable comedy as Harris asked for Portal, and the drowsy landlord, testy at being hauled out of bed after midnight, told him in well-chosen words he didn't have anyone called Portal staying at the place; in fact, he didn't have anyone staying at all, because he didn't have room, and if he did have room he would not have anyone staying there who had people who called him up at that time of night. Not for long anyway.

Harris went red, and there were some explosive exchanges before one of them slammed the receiver down. Someone slipped down and had a word with the little WAAF, and she tried in terror for the next hour to raise Washington, but without success.

. . . . . . . . . . . . . .

*Later . . .*
Ten out of the nineteen were coming home, hugging the ground, 8 tons lighter now in bomb and petrol load and travelling at maximum cruising, about 245, not worrying about petrol; only about getting home. The coast was an hour away and the sun less than that. They knew the fighters were overhead waiting for a lightening sky in the east.

Harris had driven Cochrane and Wallis to Scampton to meet the survivors, and in the ops. room at Scampton he picked up the phone to try and get Portal again. This time he prepared the ground for smart service by telling the girl that the speaker was Air Chief Marshal Sir Arthur Harris, Commander-in-Chief of Bomber Command.

'Yes, of course,' said the indulgent girl, who knew the absurd things that plastered New Zealand flight lieutenants were liable to say, 'you've been on it again, sir. Now you go and get your batman to put you to bed. He'll give you your course to steer.'

There was an explosion in the ops. room and an unusually intelligent intelligence officer hared down the stairs and told the girl the frightful thing she had done. Someone soothed the irate man in the ops. room while the girl beseeched the GPO to get Washington faster than ever before. This time the lines were clear and before long a mollified Harris had the pleasure of telling Portal, 'Operation Downwood successful . . . yes, successful!'

*The Dam Busters*, Paul Brickhill

## Boss

We lurched round West Malling again. On the next approach I brought her down lower. Too low, too slow, and always left of the runway. No good.

'Wheels up. I have the throttles. Milk the flap off gently.'

The accelerating engines roared angrily. Charlie Two crept across the dark airfield, still losing height. She gained a little airspeed in a dip beyond the runway, and clawed her way slowly up to safer air. Safer, that is, so long as there were no double-decker buses on our track.

'Jeez, skip, good job you missed that hill—we've still got the incendiaries on board.'

'What?'

'Yeah, I only dropped the HEs off in the Channel. I thought we'd save something for tomorrow.'

'You thought . . . never mind. We'll drop the lot as soon as we can find some sea.'

We slid through the black drizzle, never gaining height, found the coast and dropped a dozen canisters of fire bombs into the inky water. Plodding back to West Malling, I found that I had lost faith in the right-hand-circuit school of thought. I sat up straight, took a piece of the engineer's chewing-gum, and positioned Charlie Two for a normal left-hand circuit on the long runway.

'Okay, third time lucky. Wheels down.'

'She'll be right this time, skip.'

Charlie Two sidled down the approach, levelled out with the starboard wing down, touched starboard wheel first with a squeal, then touched the port wheel on concrete, and she was down. I found a convenient hard-standing, and switched off. Fire engines, trucks and an ambulance appeared out of the darkness. We clambered out and stood under the port wing, sheltering from the rain, and examining the blackened engines.

'That's our first abortive.'

'Who woulda thought old Charlie Two would let us down?'

'Where is this place?'

A flight truck pulled up, and from it an Irving-jacketed figure approached us. I distinguished a fair-haired man, wearing an officer's forage-cap, and moved forward to meet him. I asked:

'Are you on duty?'

'On duty? Yes. Yes, I'm on duty.'

'Right, now listen. I was here about six months ago, diverted on a night cross-country from OTU. There were no sheets on the beds, and we couldn't get a hot meal in the mess. Pretty poor show. See what you can do, will you?'

The officer's bright, blue eyes looked into mine. He smiled slightly.

'Who are you?'

'Currie—Pilot Officer Currie. I'm the captain.'

'I see. You want sheets on your beds?'

'Yes. Clean sheets.'

'And a meal?'

'Hot meals.'

'I'll see what I can do.'

'Good man.'

A truck took us to the tower, and I told the people there what had happened to Charlie Two. The intelligence officer plotted the places where we had dropped the bombs, then looked up and smiled at me.

'My God, when you came in the second time and disappeared into the dip at the end of the runway, we all put our fingers in our ears.'

'So did we.'

'By the way, did you see "Cat's-eyes"?'

'What size?'

'Cat's-eyes Cunningham—our CO.'

'No.'

'Oh, pity. He went out to meet you.'

'Oh. Not a fellow in an Irving jacket, is he?'

'That's right.'

'Oh, dear.'

Clean sheets and hot food we had, and night-fighter ace Cunningham opened the bar, and poured us a drink himself. As I told the navigator, it's always best to talk to the top man.

*Lancaster Target*, Jack Currie

# Whose Boss?

I met an amusing companion in Steve, a curly-haired, cheerful fighter pilot with a fund of good stories. Perhaps the best, and certainly the longest of these concerned one Pilot Officer Fotheringay-Jones. It seems that this paragon arrived on posting to a Spitfire squadron, and reported to the Flight Commander, a Squadron Leader Watson, who said:

'Fotheringay-Jones, eh? Jolly good show! Glad to have you with us. Now, the first thing you'll want to do is to gen up on station standing orders, station routine orders, the flight order book, pilot's notes and so on.'

'Actually, sir, no. I want to get in the air.'

'Eh?'

'In the air, sir. I want to fly a Spitfire.'

'Yes, yes, Fotheringay-Jones, of course, all in good time . . .'

'No, sir, now. I see one is ready at the hangar for air test; may I take it up?'

'Oh, very well, Fotheringay-Jones. I don't want to quench your commendable zeal. You can attend to the admin this afternoon.'

Within minutes Fotheringay-Jones was airborne. Not only airborne, but beating up the squadron offices at very low level. As the Spitfire flashed by his window for the third time, Watsson attempted to have Fotheringay-Jones recalled by Flying Control, only to find that the pilot had omitted to turn on his RT. Meanwhile, the Station Commander, Group Captain Ponsonby, was dealing with some correspondence in his headquarters, which now attracted Fotheringay-Jones's attention. As the Spitfire made his windows rattle, flashing past inverted at nought feet, the Station Commander ducked instinctively. He then picked up the telephone and directed a tirade at the unfortunate Watson for permitting such dangerous antics, and demanded an explanation.

Fotheringay-Jones eventually tired of his attempts to terrorise the station and flight commanders, and landed off a stall-turn in the circuit, flicking his wheels down at the last possible minute. As he climbed out of the cockpit, he was met by an agitated mechanic with a message from Squadron Leader Watson to report to him immediately, if not sooner.

When Fotheringay-Jones sauntered in, Watson looked at him coldly:

'I suppose you think you're very clever. You have the mistaken impression that you are an ace. Well, Fotheringay-Jones, let me tell you that you are not. You are a dangerous young fool. Had you taken the trouble to read the flight order book, as I suggested, you would have known that low flying is most strictly prohibited. As for your extraordinary behaviour in dive-bombing the admin buildings, your failure to observe RT discipline, your irregular manoeuvres in the aerodrome circuit, I shall say no more for the moment. I am bound to tell you that you have managed to incur not only my serious displeasure, but also that of the Station Commander, all within a few moments of arriving on this squadron.'

Fotheringay-Jones eyed him calmly.

'Have you quite finished, sir?'

'For the moment, yes.'

'Then you can go and get stuffed.'

'I beg your pardon?'

'Go and get stuffed.'

Watson was appalled. Dismissing Fotheringay-Jones from his presence, he reported the outcome of his interview to the Station Commander, concluding:

'I'm afraid he was rather insolent, sir.'

'What did he say?'

'I would prefer not to repeat it, sir.'

'Out with it, man!'

'Well, sir, he told me to get stuffed.'

'Did he, indeed? I can see that I shall have to deal with this fellow myself. What did you say his name was?'

'Fotheringay-Jones, sir.'

'Bring him to my office, Watson. Immediately.'

When Fotheringay-Jones had been run to earth in the bar of the officers' mess, the further interview took place, and Group Captain Ponsonby administered a similar rocket to that delivered by Squadron Leader Watson, but on a far grander scale. When he had thundered to his climax Fotheringay-Jones, who had been shuffling his feet for some time, looked up and spoke:

'Go and have a good shit.'

After a moment's horrified silence Watson, by now appalled almost to bursting point, motioned the pilot out and awaited the great man's wrath. Spluttering horribly, the Station Commander sent for Fotheringay-Jones's documents. The adjutant laid them in front of his master, who instructed Watson to read them aloud:

'Elementary Flying School—"A highly proficient student". Basic Flying School—"Well above the average". Advanced Flying School—"Exceptional". Operational Conversion Unit—"An exceptional student who will make an outstanding operational pilot". Further remarks—"Pilot Officer Fotheringay-Jones is a nephew of HM Secretary of State for Air".'

Group Captain Ponsonby knocked out his pipe in the ash-tray on his desk, and stood up purposefully:

'That will be all, Watson. For myself, I am just going to the lavatory. You, I have no doubt, will make your own arrangements.'

*Lancaster Target*, Jack Currie

# Bad Met. By Moonlight

It was Flight Lieutenant W. J. Farley who was the first to come back. This he did in a Lysander on the night of 19/20 October 1940, landing near Montigny to pick up 'Felix' (Philip Schneidau) who had parachuted in on 9/10 October. . . .

. . . On 19 October 1940, Flight Lieutenant Farley was at Tangmere, frustrated by the bad weather. Well aware of how impatiently Philip would be expecting him, he pleaded with the commanding officer at Tangmere to let him have a crack at the operation, in spite of the bad weather. It was finally agreed that he could, but that, if the weather was still bad over the French coast, he would turn back. He took off from Tangmere in pouring rain which soaked the radio set in the back. The sliding roof over the rear cockpit had been removed to make it easier for Philip to climb in.

The weather was better over France and Farley found the field south of

Fontainebleau. As arranged, Philip switched on the inverted 'L' shaped pattern of lights which he had designed with Farley on a tablecloth in Oddenino's restaurant—the basic flarepath design for a Lysander pick-up landing which never needed to be improved throughout the war. Farley landed at 0117 and taxied back to the first lamp. Philip climbed up the fixed exterior ladder, which he had designed, and Farley took off. After taking off he remarked that there was something jamming the free movement of the elevator. He throttled back until he could clear it, losing a little height. At this moment Philip believes that a bullet went through the compass between Farley's knees. This must have been fired by the sentry outside the CO's villa in the neighbouring village of Marlotte. For some time Farley could see to map-read by moonlight but then the cloud built up. Climbing to 16,000 feet they were still in cloud with no navigation aid at all, not even a compass. The wireless was too wet to work and the rear cockpit, with no canopy, was bitterly cold. Over the French coast the weather was just as foul as it had been when Farley had taken off from Tangmere. There was a south-westerly gale blowing and Farley was afraid that they might be drifting over Belgium or Holland. They were completely lost but they plodded on and on. Farley told Philip to look out for any sight of land, especially if there was any field visible which offered the possibility of a forced landing.

At about 0630 Farley said that the petrol tanks had been indicating 'empty' for some time and that 'JC must be doing His stuff' to keep them airborne. At 0650 Philip reported seeing some land along the top of some cliffs where a landing might be possible. 'Good-oh! Then we'll go down', said Farley. Then he said that it might be the North German coast. Philip said that, 'when a nipper', he had read a book called *The Riddle of the Sands* and so this could not be the North German coast. With cliffs like that Philip guessed that it might be the West Irish coast. At this point the petrol finally ran dry. They glided down and, when about 50 feet up, they observed that the ground above the cliffs had been planted with pine posts to stop enemy aircraft landing there. Farley told Philip to lie down before the landing because there was a danger of a post folding back a wing in such a way that it would chop off his head if he sat up.

Farley also told Philip to take all his clothes off as he was dressed as a civilian and they might be in enemy occupied territory. Philip did this and—at 0655—they hit the ground. The wings came off as predicted. Philip thrust all his clothes into a haversack with two bottles of brandy and, stark naked, jumped out of the wreck of the Lysander, clutching the haversack. He ran round to the front saying: 'Wally, get out! This will catch fire'. Farley replied: 'If there's one thing this won't do it's catch fire. There's no f . . . ing petrol'. Farley climbed out and set off, saying that he would look for help. If he came back with help he would raise his right arm. Otherwise Philip should throw everything into the sea. To be ready to do this he should now go to the top of the cliff.

Ten minutes later Farley reappeared with two enormous men. Philip was glad to see that their rifles were slung over their left shoulders. He hastily put on his underclothes and went to meet them. Farley said: 'I can't understand a word they are saying, but it appears we are in Scotland'. They were invited to a hastily prepared but substantial breakfast which neither of

them could eat. RAF Oban, which was nearby, was telephoned and the RAF police soon arrived to collect two obvious spies.

They were brought before the station commander of this RAF Coastal Command Station. He quite reasonably asked them who they were and what they had been doing. Farley confined himself to giving his name and number. Philip said that they had been doing a special recce over the Atlantic but that he was not allowed to give his name. This did not seem to humour the station commander. Faced with almost total lack of co-operation, he put them under armed guard in a bed-room—where they found the beds very much to their liking. Meanwhile the officer in charge of this operation, a naval lieutenant, had arranged to borrow an aircraft from the Fleet Air Arm station at Ford to patrol the Channel to look for the wreckage of the Lysander. I suppose nobody had told him that a ditched Lysander sinks instantly. After an hour and a half they were told that a Lysander had crashed six miles north of Oban. The first reaction was that it could not possibly be the Lysander they were looking for. When they later heard that the pilot's name was Farley, they incredulously called off the search. So, on 20 October 1940, ended the first clandestine pick-up operation of World War Two.

*We Landed by Moonlight*, Hugh Verity

## RAF POWs march East into Germany ahead of Allied Advance, 1943

Now that we were across the Elbe, our high spirits were somewhat modified, in spite of the fact that the Allies were already across the river a hundred miles to the south, and we settled down to a few more weeks of captivity.

Midday on the day following our river crossing, we were sitting down by the roadside, indulging in a five minutes halt.

'John, come here quick,' came George's voice from a gate on the other side of the road.

I got up, leaving my pack and overcoat by the roadside, and followed him through the gate to a small farmhouse.

'Look at this Johnnie, it's just what you want.'

George had led me to a small open barn, and pointed out a very diminutive doll's pram, which was painted yellow, and in rather a dilapidated condition.

'Bit small isn't it?' I said.

The pram was about 2 feet 6 inches long, and 18 inches high.

'Well, hell! It's better than nothing and has four strong wheels,' he answered.

'I'll try,' I said, and rapped on the door of the house.

A woman came to the door, and I said in German: 'You have a doll's pram, and I would like to buy it. I have some real coffee.'

Her eyes lit up at the magic word 'Kaffee', and she came with me to the barn.

'Of course it's not a very good pram,' I remarked, 'so I can't give you very much coffee.'

We settled for four heaped teaspoonfuls of American Nescafé, and I proudly wheeled my vehicle out into the road.

I was greeted by a hoot of laughter.

Ignoring the rude comments, I loaded on my pack and overcoat, which just managed to fit inside. The column moved on, and I started to push, bent almost double in order to reach down to the 18-inch-high handle.

After five minutes I realized that this method of propulsion would not do at all. Some other means had to be devised. I tied a strip of sheet to the handle, and started pulling, but the wretched vehicle would not keep straight.

I stopped by the roadside and cut a 6-foot length of sapling which I lashed to one of the springs with the strip of sheet.

For about two miles I struggled along the road, pulling the pram, endeavouring to catch up with my own block.

'Oh, blast the thing!' I shouted, as a front wheel came off, the pram overturned and dumped all my stuff into the road. The column marched by relentlessly, and I was assailed by grins and fatuous suggestions.

There was nothing for it but to don my overcoat, shoulder my pack and carry the damned pram, as the clip which fixed the wheel to the axle had broken.

Luckily for me the journey's end was only about three miles away. I arrived at our camping site in a state of complete exhaustion, still carrying the pram.

*Final Flight*, J. Hartnell-Beavis

## St Omer, France, 9 August 1941

Three German soldiers in grey uniforms were bending over him, taking off his harness and Mae West. No one spoke that he remembered. They picked him up and carried him to a car in a lane, feeling nothing, neither pain nor thought, only a dazed quiescence. The car moved off and he saw fields through the windows but did not think of anything. After timeless miles there were houses and the car rumbled over the *pavé*, through the arch of a gateway to a grey stone building. The Germans lifted him out and carried him through a door up some steps and along a corridor . . . he smelt the familiar hospital smell . . . into a bare, aseptic room, and then they were laying him on a padded casualty table. Old memories stirred. A thinnish man in a white coat and rimless glasses walked up and looked down at him. A girl in nurse's uniform hovered behind.

The doctor frowned at the empty trouser leg, pulled the torn cloth aside and stared in amazement, then looked at Bader's face and at the wings and medal ribbons on his tunic. Puzzled he said: 'You have lost your leg.'

Bader spoke for the first time since the enemy had hit him. 'Yes, it came off as I was getting out of my aeroplane.'

The doctor looked at the stump again, trying to equate a one-legged man with a fighter pilot. 'Ach, so!' he said obviously. 'It is an old injury,' and joked mildly. 'You seem to have lost both your legs—your real one and your artificial one.'

Bader thought: God, you haven't seen anything yet. He waited with a grim and passive curiosity for the real joke.

'You have cut your throat,' the doctor said. He put his hand up and was surprised to feel a large gash under his chin, sticky with blood. It did not hurt.

The doctor peered at it, then stuck his fingers between the teeth and felt round the floor of the mouth. Light-headed, Bader felt a sudden horror that the cut might have gone right through. For some absurd reason that mattered terribly. But apparently it was all right.

'I must sew this up,' the doctor murmured. He jabbed a syringe near the gash and the area went numb. No one spoke while he stitched the lips of the gash.

'Now we must have your trousers off and see your leg,' he said.

Bader thought: This is going to be good, and raised his rump a little as the doctor unbuttoned the trousers and eased them down over the hips. The doctor froze, staring transfixed at the leather and metal that encased the stump of the left leg. There was a silence.

At last he noisily sucked in a breath, and said 'Ach!' He looked once more at Bader, back at the two stumps and again at Bader, and said in a voice of sober discovery: 'We have heard about you.'

*Reach for the Sky*, Paul Brickhill

## The Young Bomber, Iraq, 1923

During our stay at Mosul the squadron lived in a small detached mess consisting of only a few rooms, in which we were very cramped. I shared a room with Harris and Saundby which the squadron also used for recreational purposes, as it was the only one with a fireplace and the weather was bitterly cold.

One evening our fire started smoking badly. When Harris got up and went outside, he discovered that someone had put a wet sack over the chimney pot, and a few minutes later there was a loud explosion as two revolver cartridges went off in the fire and blew showers of sparks and lumps of burning wood into the room. Harris took no notice at the time, but about an hour later, it would then have been about 10.30 PM, he turned to me and said, 'Basil, tell Beardsworth I want him.'

When Beardsworth reported, Harris said, 'Beardsworth, I want you to go to the airfield and see if the aeroplanes are picketed down securely, because my chimney has been smoking badly and I think the wind must have got up. When you return, come and tell me if all is in order.'

Beardsworth asked, 'May I have transport, sir, because the airfield is about a mile away?'

'No!'

When Beardsworth returned and reported all was well, Harris said, 'Tell Jacques I want him.'

He gave Jacques similar instructions, and when he returned to report said, 'Tell Rodwell I want him.'

When Rodwell was given the same orders, he said, 'But, sir, Jacques has just returned from the airfield and reported that all the aeroplanes are absolutely secure.'

'Do as you are told,' snapped Harris. When Rodwell returned it must have been nearly 1 AM, but Harris repeated the whole performance, this time asking for a map to be brought from his tented office on the airfield by each offender in turn. No one ever tried that sort of joke on Harris again!

*Mission Completed*, Sir Basil Embry

## In Persona, in Absentia, Inextricable

Pilot Officer Percy Prune was famous in the war-time Royal Air Force, in fact he came to be as well-known as any of the aces but, whereas their renown came through achievement, Prune's notoriety was for non-achievement—or, more often, for achievement in the wrong direction and he was not so much well-known as notorious.

He was the fool, the poop, the boob, the mug, the mutt, the butt, the clot, the affable dim-wit of the RAF. Fatuously exuberant yet permanently bone-headed, he invariably made a muck of everything he set out to do. And yet survived to make another. From the smoking wreckage of his latest 'prunery', miraculously as safe as ever, he contemplated with a hurt and puzzled detachment the incomprehensible eccentricities of a world which was never quite within his grasp; a world in which undercarriages never came down of their own accord before his landings, and he never understood why—a world in which his famous finger went unerringly to the wrong 'tit'. Prune tried, but never learned. He was willing, but wet. He was dutiful but dumb. He was one in a thousand—nay a million. He can be hailed as 'one of the Few', the very few, which was as well for the Allied Air Forces and the RAF in particular.

Percy Prune, PO, had an answer for everything and was a master of what the RAF called the 'line-shoot'. Those violent ploughings-in of his aircraft, in flashes of fire and clouds of smoke and dust, which brought fire-tender and red-crossed 'blood wagons' speeding across the war-time

Once again PO Prune's navigation has enabled him to spend Xmas away.
*Tee Emm*, January 1944

aerodromes, were regarded by Prune as 'perfect three-point' landings—'two wheels and a nose!'

Serving in Bomber Command, he was heard over his radio to remark to his crew during a pause in his singing of dirty songs (*and* when an overall order for radio silence was in force) 'Southend is very noisy tonight'. At that moment he was passing over the Coastal Defences of Occupied France. On his return from a raid on Ludwigsburg (at the briefing everybody else had understood that the target for that night was Pfullendorf (but Prune said that he couldn't spell that), he said the flak was so thick that—'just for a lark, I selected wheels down and actually made a temporary landing on it'.

He had the normal operational pilot's disdain for 'top brass' and on seeing a visiting Air Vice Marshal in the mess, a gentleman whose cap was covered with 'scrambled egg' and whose left breast bore a five-decker set of 'fruit salad', Prune said 'I'll bet he's been in the Air Force since Pontius was a pilot'.

Not everybody in the RAF was certain that in fact Prune *was* an imaginary person—after all there was 'proof of his existence contained in the secret, official, telephone directory of the Air Ministry because, dead-pan, the Editor of *Tee Emm*, Anthony Armstrong, had told a humourless Civil Servant, who was helping to compile the directory, that the vacant chair and desk in his office (provided for Bill Hooper whenever he came off-Squadron to do some cartoons) was that of 'Pilot Officer P. Prune, Special Duties Branch' and this duly appeared in the official directory. After this a variety of people telephoned his number—including 'The Chief', Lord Arthur Tedder, Marshal of the Royal Air Force. Usually these enquiries were answered by Squadron Leader A. A. Willis who would say that Prune was not yet back from lunch and when a certain 'Waaf Queen', who was making a list of people for a cocktail party, said that it was not yet midday, Willis countered with 'Ah, but I mean *yesterday's* lunch'.

*The Passing of Pilot Officer Prune*,
Bill Hooper

OF COURSE THIS DIDN'T HAPPEN REALLY

'Pilot Officer Prune, please!'

*Tee Emm*, January 1946

# Gardez l'Eau

. . . during a GH training exercise Dig asked Les to take over the controls while he went to the Elsan. I can't remember why he asked Les to fly, but it

PO Prune's definition of a good landing is one you can walk away from.
*Tee Emm*, January 1943

was a crazy request. Les had never touched a control column in his life and knew as much about piloting as about the second coming of Christ. When he and Dig changed places his parachute harness fouled the throttles and we began to skate erratically across the sky, but finally he was installed in the pilot's seat and after being assured by Dig that the aircraft was on 'automatic pilot' and a beaut to fly, he was left in charge.

A fore and aft movement was instantly discernible; the aircraft might have been a dinghy gently riding an ocean swell. Harry, whose knowledge of piloting, or parousia for that matter, was on a par with Les's, began to issue agitated instructions from the tail. The motion became increasingly violent and I wondered whether Dig would be able to scramble over the flapjack and main bulkhead on his return journey. It was a tremendous relief to hear his voice on the intercom again and feel the aircraft respond to his sure touch.

After landing I told Dig that we couldn't go through a tour of operations with him having a slash in the back while someone up front tried to hang the kite to a nail in the sky.

Les, who was listening, endorsed this opinion with the conviction of a man who can argue from hard experience. 'I agree with Mike,' he said. 'I was shit-scared when you told me to take over.'

Dig asked us to suggest an alternative.

'Take a pot,' I said.

'I'm not taking a bloody pot . . . Anyway, who would empty it?'

But he relented, and for the next flight arrived with a large tin that had once contained fruit. He said, 'This is my can,' and from then on this article of utility was known as 'Dig's can' and went everywhere with us. It was my job to empty the can down the 'window' chute after use.

*The Eighth Passenger*, Miles Tripp

## English Spoken, RAF Kenley, 1940

'I remember a gaping hole appearing in the bottom of the cockpit. The entire radiator had been shot away, and I knew it was just a matter of time before the engine would seize, so I put my finger on the trigger and kept it there until my guns stopped firing. By that time he had both his engines on fire and I was blazing quite merrily too. I think it was a glycol fire rather than an oil fire, but *what* was burning didn't particularly interest me: I knew that *I* was burning and I was going to have to get out.

'As soon as the guns ran out of ammunition, by which time the He. III was diving steeply through the cloud, I left the aircraft.

'I came out of cloud in time to see my aircraft dive into the ground and explode. While drifting down, I saw various people running across the fields to where it had crashed. There was one man passing almost underneath me, when I was about five hundred feet up, so I shouted. This chap stopped and looked in all directions, so I shouted again, "Right above you." He looked up, and I saw that he was a Home Guard.

'As he saw me, he raised a double-barrelled shotgun to his shoulder and took aim. I knew it was a double-barrelled shotgun, because I was looking down the barrels; and they looked like twin railway tunnels!

'I shouted, "For God's sake don't shoot," and amplified it with a lot of Anglo-Saxon words that I happened to know, and continued to exhort him not to shoot for the rest of my way down; and added a lot more Anglo-Saxon words.

'Eventually I fell in a field and just sat there, but he still kept me covered with this gun. I said "Hang on a minute, while I get at my pocket and show you my identity card." He put his gun down and said, "I don't want to see your identity card: anyone who can swear like that couldn't possibly be German."'

*Ginger Lacey, Fighter Pilot*,
Richard Townshend Bickers

## Spitfire Passengers
## 1. No 111 Squadron, North Africa, 1942

After a struggle in which all hands took part, we managed to drag the last Spitfire out of the mud. In the afternoon we were called upon to escort some

Hurribombers to Mateur, but previously I had carried out some taxying trials on the wire mesh runways, and found it necessary to carry an airman on the tail to prevent the aircraft tipping onto its nose, until the moment of take-off, when we waved him off. When the squadron had just got airborne in a left-hand circuit, I looked back to see to my horror that Tommy Tinsey still had his man pinned to his empennage and his aircraft bucking like a wild west bronco. He must have forgotten to wave him away. When I warned him of the predicament on the RT, he answered that he was well aware of it, and couldn't 'shake the bugger off'.

I told him to make a landing with plenty of speed to prevent stalling, which he managed precariously to accomplish. The airman was tossed off on making contact with the ground, and got away with only a broken leg.

That evening I drank a quarter of a bottle of whisky before I tore Tinsey off a monumental strip for carelessness, and threatened to kick him out of the squadron. This had been only one of a succession of his 'blacks' and ill-discipline, but he promised to reform so I forgave him.

The airman became quite a hero to his mates, and was delighted to be invalided out of the front line.

## 2. England, 1942

On October 14th, Humphrey had flown to Worthydown a light plane to pick me up for a party of his in London. We had a few drinks with Larry and Vivien in the Ladies Room of the Officers' Mess after which we repaired to the aircraft but found that we couldn't start the motor owing to some mechanical failure. We looked at one another and then simultaneously at the Spitfire I had just finished testing. There was only one alternative. We had to make the party. Humphrey got in, and I sat on his lap. We couldn't use straps, or close the hood. Neither could one of us handle all the controls. I took the stick, the throttle and right rudder, Humphrey the left, the pitch and the undercarriage lever. We opened up and staggered into the air. Immediately, we realised that we were in dead trouble, and I tried to get my left foot onto the other pedal. In the attempt, I kicked the stick forward which bucked the aircraft and shot me outwards. Humphrey grabbed, and hauled me back into the cockpit. We decided we'd have to let things be. When we got to Heston, we both knew there could be no 'going round again'. We motored in, and made a passable landing. I jumped out and Humphrey taxied in. When he had switched off, we solemnly swore that we would never try tandem again.

We had hardly ordered our first drink when an apoplectic Station Commander attacked us. 'What in the hell do you think you're doing?' he bellowed. 'I'll have you court-martialled for this.'

It transpired that the stupefied flying controller, when asked the name of the pilot, had replied: 'There were two, Sir.' Fortunately, the Station Commander was a veteran of the last war, and six double gins later, we were forgiven, but banned from ever landing at Heston again.

During November, I got an urgent call from Gordon Brettel. He was being court-martialled for flying a WAAF on his lap to a dance in a Spitfire. One of the three charges was endangering the King's aircraft, for which he could expect a severe penalty. He asked me if I would testify in his defence. I said I would, and to expect me at Biggin where he was stationed with 92 Squadron.

I explained my friend's predicament to Jeffrey Quill and Joe Smith, our chief designer at Supermarines, and Joe agreed to write me out some mathematical equations relating to centres of gravity which no one would understand and which would prove irrefutably that the King's aircraft was never in any danger, subject to knowing the size of the young lady. I was able to give this from personal experience, that her dimensions, although substantial, would not interfere with the controls of the aircraft.

I produced this evidence at the court-martial and the prosecuting counsel asked how I could prove it. 'I've done it', I said, 'and if the Court so pleases, I'd be happy to fly prosecuting counsel on my lap.' The court hastily recessed—counsel declined, and Gordon Brettel was acquitted on that charge.

*From the Journals of a Fighter Pilot,*
Anthony Bartley

## Duty Free, No 92 Squadron, RAF Northolt, 1940

The third week in May, a section of three led by Paddy Green, my flight commander, escorted Churchill and his Chiefs of Staff in a Flamingo to and from Paris on a last resort mission to try and bolster French morale before their capitulation. I did not consider that there was any possibility of contact with the enemy, so, before leaving Le Bourget, I unloaded the ammunition from one of my machine gun tanks and substituted bottles of brandy. On landing back at Northolt, mission accomplished, my armourers, according to standard operational procedure, whipped open the ammunition bays to check re-armament, and my precious bottles broke on contact with the tarmac.

The PM, who had just disembarked from his Flamingo parked beside me, witnessed my despondency, let alone concern about court martial, walked over to me, opened his top coat, and from its pockets produced two bottles of the same brand.

All he said was, 'Smart thinking, young man. It was the last chance either of us is going to get.'

With that, I knew my transgression would never be reported beyond the perimeter track of Northolt airfield.

*From the Journals of a Fighter Pilot,*
Anthony Bartley

# Cartoons

The Theory of Flight

School of Technical Training,
RAF Hednesford, 1942

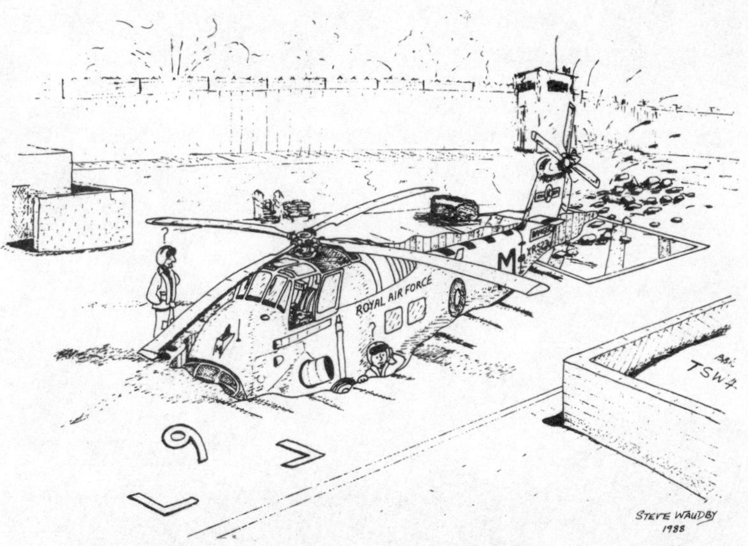


'I think you need to bring the power in a little bit earlier, mate!'
[Slight exaggeration of an incident at Bessbrook on 3 February 1988]

Steve Waudby, 1988

'Wot yer moanin' about? Fits yer like a glove, chum—covers yer 'ands, don't it?'

Fisher, *Laugh with SEAC*, 1945

'I wonder if you can tell me if the "Pension Rosa" at Baden-Baden is still unscathed?'

Frank Reynolds, *Punch*

'. . . As I was saying just before we took off . . .'

Brockbank, *Punch*

'There 'e goes again, Sir—Muvver's little bahnsin' boy!'

'What are you doing out here—got claustrophobia or something?'

Sillince, *Punch*

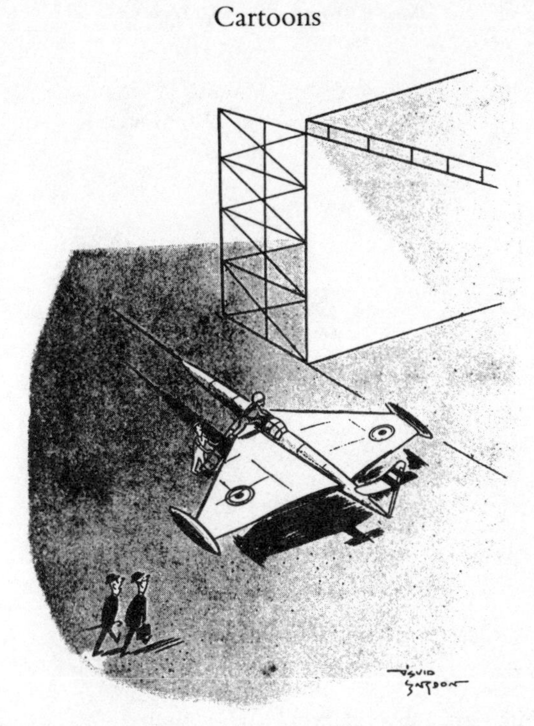

'Shall we mention it's scrapped *before* he flight-tests it?'
David Langdon, 1957

'Same damn trouble every time—never anyone left to give ME a shove.'
David Langdon, 1945

'Have a word with Carter about improving his sprinting—otherwise we'll have to ground him'

Brockbank, 1943

'Right—right—left—steady—steady . . .'

Maskee, 1944

'I WISH I could remember whether the red goes inside or outside.'

Hickey

'Yes, I think that $\frac{3}{16}$ nut on the starboard outer's prop spinner's okay now, Corp.'

David Langdon, 1945

'I'm afraid we shall have to leave building the new wing until after the war.'
1943

Parachute inventor to airman: 'Now do your very best. If it doesn't open, I'm ruined.'
Frank R. Grey, 1932

'I think it's wonderful how the little ones manage to keep up with the big ones.'
Sillince

'Right! Now we've got that little lot off, what's the trouble with your bike?'
David Langdon, 1944

'I was in the Air Force when petrol bowsers were horse-drawn.'

D. G. K.

'Forty odd years ago they were known as the "Brylcreem Boys".'

D. G. K.

# DON'T FORGET YOUR MAE WEST, SHE HASN'T FORGOTTEN YOU!

*The following letter from Miss Mae West has reached* TEE EMM. *Miss West saw a paragraph in a Los Angeles paper suggesting that the name "Mae West" for the R.A.F. life-saving jacket might soon get into the dictionary.*

Brent Productions.]

*A Mae West.*

*THE Mae West.*

DEAR BOYS OF THE R.A.F.,

I have just seen that the R.A.F. flyers have a life-saving jacket they call a "Mae West," because it bulges in all the "right places." Well, I consider it a swell honour to have such great guys wrapped up in you, know what I mean?

Yes, it's kind of a nice thought to be flying all over with brave men . . . even if I'm only there by proxy in the form of a life-saving jacket, or a life-saving jacket in my form.

I always thought that the best way to hold a man was in your arms—but I guess when you're up in the air a plane is safer. You've got to keep everything under control.

Yeah, the jacket idea is all right, and I can't imagine anything better than to bring you boys of the R.A.F. soft and happy landings. But what I'd like to know about that life-saving jacket is—has it got dangerous curves and soft shapely shoulders?

You've heard of Helen of Troy, the dame with the face that launched a thousand ships . . . why not a shape that will stop thousands of tanks?

If I do get in the dictionary—where you say you want to put me—how will they describe me? As a warm and clinging life-saving garment worn by aviators? Or an aviator's jacket that supplies the woman's touch while the boys are flying around nights? How would you describe me, boys?

I've been in *Who's Who*, and I know what's what, but it'll be the first time I ever made the dictionary.

Sin-sationally,

Mae West

*Tee Emm*, January 1942

**Service Terms Illustrated
by well-known newspaper cartoonists**

**No. 1 Pathfinders**
Wyndham Robinson of *The Star*

*Tee Emm*, February 1943

**No. 8 'Tearing off a Strip'**
Lee of *The Evening News*

*Tee Emm*, September 1943

'Why *I* must buy everyone else a drink every time *I* shoot down a wretched Hun, is something I can never understand.'

David Langdon, *Punch*

'Faster, boys—its the only bit of shade we may see for weeks.'

Fitz, *Punch*

## The Seven Deadly Sins of Navigators

**No. 1 Ignoring Wind Effect**
Roberts, *Tee Emm*, August 1945

**No. 3 Inability to Clear Stoppages**
Roberts, *Tee Emm*, March 1945

**No. 6 Being Surprised**

Roberts, *Tee Emm*, June 1945

**No. 7 Failure to Acknowledge Recall Signal**

Roberts, *Tee Emm*, October 1944

'Flight Sergeant said: "Go and give 'em a hand in the cookhouse." Trouble is I don't know the first thing about cooking.'

David Langdon, *Punch*

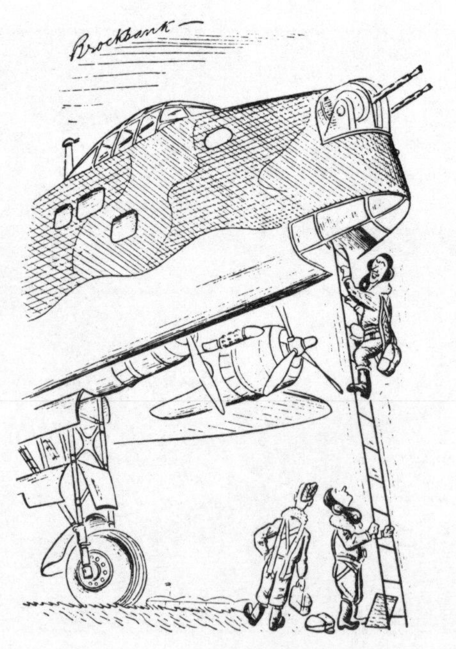

'Of course, I'm all right when it's in the air; it's climbing into it that makes me dizzy.'

Brockbank, *Punch*

'I've worked it out that, allowing for speed variation, wind and surface resistance and what not, we can get across the runway before that kite, with approximately a yard to spare . . .'

David Langdon, *Punch*

'What's wrong with this chap?'

David Langdon, 1968

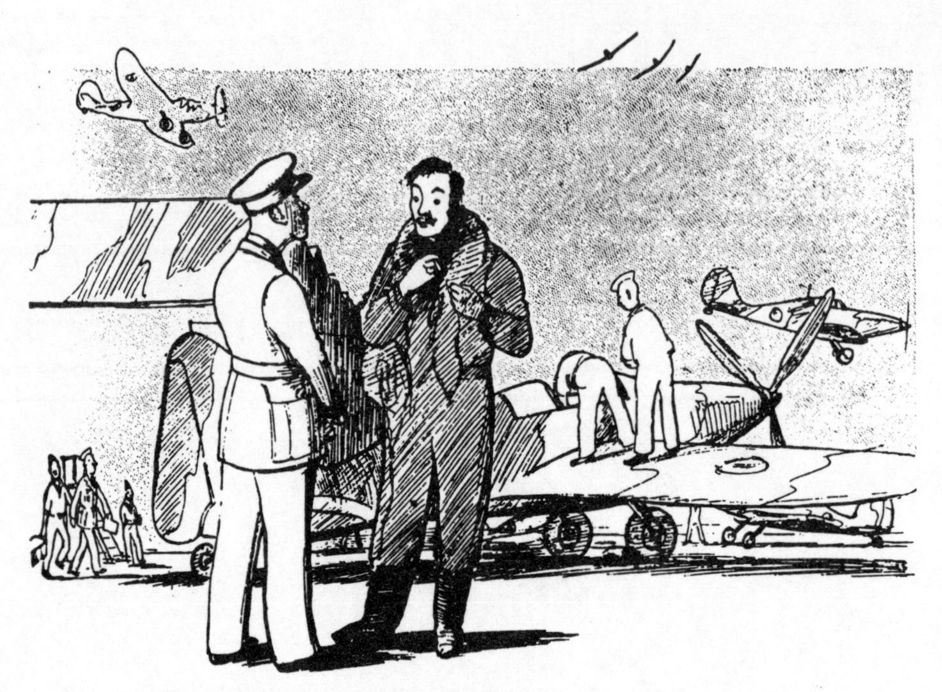

'But you must remember that I outnumbered them by one to three.'
Pont, 1940

'Orderly Officer. Any complaints?'
David Langdon

'Who is flying this damn thing?'

Kane

'Whad'ya mean, "Where's the Marine Craft Section?" This is it!'

Kane

'When's it due for a primary, Chiefy?'

Kane

'If we cop it, don't let that new bombsight fall into enemy hands.'

Bill Tidy

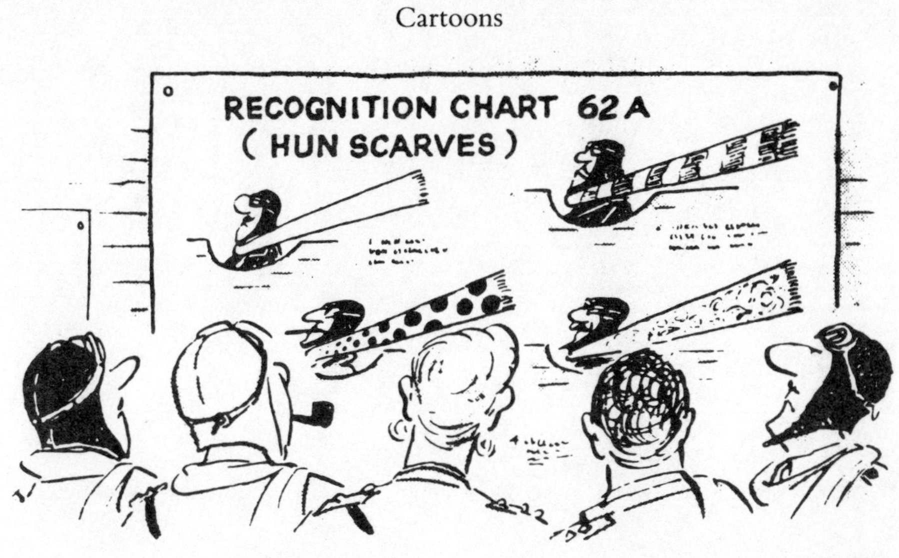


Bill Tidy

'As soon as he looks the other way, you hop over the wire . . .'

# Linebooks

## No 1 Squadron Linebook

**1966**
'I was flying before the Dead Sea reported sick.'

**1982**
On copying a complex low-level route: 'This route makes the wiring diagram of a microchip look simple.'

**1988**
On discussing how he had been intercepted by Swiss F5s whilst en route to an airshow in Switzerland: 'I was very impressed: apart from the Flight Plan they didn't even know I was coming.'

**1988**
During a ship-recognition lecture, after discussing a heavily defended Soviet cruiser: 'That's the sort of mission the JPs [junior pilots] would be leading.'

## No 6 Squadron Linebook

**1988**
The squadron was deployed to the Royal Danish Air Force Base, Tirstrup, and the pilots were gathered outside a tent, chatting over a beer or three. A nameless squadron leader Flight Commander had changed and was wearing a rather becoming T-shirt emblazoned 'Pratt and Whitney' (makers of jet engines!). At a suitable lull in conversation, a squadron pilot interjected: 'Hey OC B, I didn't know your wife was called Whitney.'

## No 10 Squadron Linebook

Flying in the Middle East in the 1970s, a No 10 Squadron crew passed an Aeroflot crew climbing out of Aden.

Aeroflot (heavily accented): 'You British Royal Air Force? You used to have Aden?'

No 10 Squadron: 'Yes.'

Aeroflot: 'Well, we just had to nightstop there and we would like you to have it back.'

A British Airways pilot waiting to taxi at Heathrow watched a No 10 Squadron aircraft cross in front of him with Mrs Thatcher on board and, referring to his Company's unkind name of our elegant jet, transmitted 'Quack, Quack. The Iron Lady in the Iron Duck!'

## No 11 Squadron Linebook

**1958**
Wing Commander Flying, asking Taff Wallis a sample question that the Air Officer Commanding may ask on the history of No 11 Squadron:

Wing Commander: 'How many aircraft did 11 Squadron shoot down during the last war?'

Taff: 'None, I shouldn't think!'

Wing Commander: 'Hmph! I shot down three myself.'

Overheard in crewroom: 'That formation we did on the weather check was a sight better than that flypast and I took off eating a meat pie!'

**1972**
Duty Authorizer to Duty Pilot

'Can you see the wind sock yet?'

'Yes.'

'OK, let him go!'

## No 18 Squadron Linebook

**Mid-1960s**
Spoken by ex-wartime master pilot on the subject of being requested to donate blood to the German Blood Bank: 'They tried to get my blood twenty years ago, they're not getting it now!'

Conversation overheard between a Master Pilot and an Air Cadet:

Cadet: 'Excuse me, sir, but are you a pilot?'

M. Pilot: 'Yes.'

Cadet: 'But I thought the lowest aircrew rank was Pilot Officer.'

M. Pilot: 'It is!'

**1976**
Overheard on Approach Frequency:

Pilot: 'OK, Gary, you've got the Frankfurt continuous voice weather broadcast on the radio.'

Co-Pilot: 'Roger, are you going to speak to them or shall I?'

## No 19 Squadron Linebook

US Pilot: 'God, I'm tired.'

RAF Pilot: 'Yeah, you look about as sharp as the leading edge of a fog bank!'

Scene: Squadron junior boys driving around local German town in a Royal Air Force 4-ton truck, dressed up as a pirate ship, looking for the rest of the German Carnival floats, already half an hour late. Finally the truck stops:

Anon: 'I'm sure this is the right place—it's just that nobody else seems to be here.'

## No 27 Squadron Linebook

Scene: A flying instructor (QFI) who prides himself with being one of the smoothest landers on the Squadron, prepares himself to descend.

QFI: 'Hey, kid, this is going to be one of my smoothest ever landings.'

. . . after a rather firm return to terra firma . . .

NAV: 'That wasn't very smooth.'

QFI: 'No, kid, the landing was smooth, but the runway is bumpy.'

During a discussion about the Falklands, one Squadron member was heard to say: 'My claim to fame is that I trained the crew that missed the runway (at Stanley).'

Buccaneer Nav to Tornado Nav: 'Your kit is like our pilots—it gets the blame when things go wrong.'

## No 32 Squadron Linebook

**1941–5**

Russel is the head of International 32.
He leads the boys around the sky and shows them what to do.
One day while shooting Messerschmitts one crept up from the rear—thereafter Humphrey went on leave, and stayed there half a year.

Hector's head of 'A' Flight and has got the DFC
For shooting down a dozen Huns, a grand show you'll agree.
With iron hand in velvet glove he rules his little troup.
And by far his favourite target (next to Messerschmitts) is Group.

Then comed old Falkowaski, who leads the Polish stars.
His English is quite good, though somewhat different from ours.
While shooting down a Hun one night, his engine coughed and failed,
He shouted loudly 'Kurva Jegomasz!' and out he baled.

Next to him comes Voski, who's another happy lad.
His manners are perfection, and his English far from bad.
When out with him at parties be sure to stick to beer
Or he'll fix you up with 'specials', and ruin your career.

**1948**
The Flak was so thick you could lower your undercarriage and taxi over it.

**1951**
Felt the wheels touch, so I logged a heavy landing.

**1953**
After an air to ground sortie, on hearing his score was forty-seven hits out of fifty rounds fired, Flight Sergeant Smith was heard to remark in a puzzled voice, 'I wonder what happened to the other three rounds.'

**June 1984**
The Air Officer Commanding, Air Vice Marshal P—, flying the HS 125 to Aldergrove for his annual inspection, when advised that he was currently some four minutes late and it was necessary to keep the speed up for an on-time arrival, replied, 'It's all right, they can't start without me.'

# No 33 Squadron Linebook

**1973**
Weather report for Leeming passed by Odiham Met Office: 'Vertical visibility zero.'

Pilot: 'Is that in feet or metres?'

**1977**
A flight lieutenant reflecting on his life as a pilot: '. . . long periods of inactivity, interjected with moments of sheer terror, (pause) for which I receive flying pay.'

**1983**
VIP trip from Odiham to Fleetlands with an Air Marshal at the controls. The aircraft finally arrived at Fleetlands and landed (sort of!).

Air Marshal: 'Oh dear, I don't think I'll ever make a helicopter pilot.'

Squadron Pilot: 'I wouldn't worry, sir . . . I'll never make an Air Marshal!'

**1986**
Aircrew briefing room prior to brief for helicopter flying display:

Pilot: 'Well, shall we just go through the display routine?'

Crewman: 'Well, I thought I'd just do the usual thing on start up and hang on tight for the rest of the flight!'

# No 41 Squadron Linebook

**1973**

A squadron leader after having to stop taxying to have the aircraft steps retracted: 'Flying with the steps down is no problem until you go low level.'

The bright-tailed and bushy-eyed pilot was prostrate in a small Cyprus hotel after a memorable Saturday:

'I'm glad I'm not a tee-totaller.'

'Why's that?'

'Imagine waking up to the knowledge that this is the best you are going to feel all day.'

The Senior Engineering Officer telephoned Operations (he thought) to organize snow clearing of the squadron dispersal:

Voice: ''ello.'

S. Eng. O: 'Do you speak English?'

Voice: 'Yes.'

S. Eng. O: 'Right—I want the area in front of hangar Bravo and the 41 Sqn shelters cleared by 0630 hours.'

Voice: 'This is the Base Commander in his home—I suggest you contact Ops!'

Passing an aerial farm on a bus ride to HMS *Terror*, Singapore:

Tanker Pilot: 'How would you count the masts in a thing like that?'

Squadron Pilot: 'Well, the navigator has a rod, with beads on it, and he slides one along for each mast he sees. Then he passes it up front to be counted.'

# No 43 Squadron Linebook

**1959**

Bill said that Lossie were flying with an aircraft carrier as their No 1 diversion . . . 'the *Glorious* or something.'

Jock Heron: 'Nonsense, that sank years ago.'
Chris: 'OK, so it's a lousy diversion.'

**1978**

Squadron Leader Coville, having returned from Tactical Fighter Meet, was interrupted in his soliloquy by a pair of the notoriously short-ranged Lightnings taking off. 'Is it worth my while continuing, because they'll be back before I'm finished.'

After a telephone enquiry from the newly-opened Battle of Britain museum:

Wildpig: 'Was 43 still serving at Tangmere at 10.30 AM on 11 Sept 1940?'

Pete: 'Why, has there been a low-flying complaint?'

**1979**

In Cyprus at a shopping centre, during Armaments Practice Camp (APC):

Small Boy: 'Are you a fighter pilot, mister?'

Al: 'Sure am, sonny.'

Small Boy: 'I am going to grow up and I am going to be a fighter pilot.'

Al: 'Well, you can do one or the other, son, but you can't do both.'

**1986**

Night dual check time:

Steve Carr: 'Do you want to do your night dual check tonight?'

Sach: 'Hell no, its getting really dark out there.'

Senior Medical Officer (SMO) in crew room just before trip.

SMO: 'You know, I'm the only non-aircrew person on the station who's able to get a flying suit on issue. It says so in QRs.'

Pilot: 'You know you're the only person on the station in a green suit who has time to read QRs.'

Boys in downtown Limassol after a heavy night in the bar are accosted by random local.

Random Local: 'Hey, you buy Cyprus wines, very good, very cheap, best on island?'

Boys: 'Nah, gives us a headache.'

Random Local: 'Is OK, we sell you aspirin.'

## No 70 Squadron Linebook

**1978**

Crew member reflecting on a trip to the United States: 'Las Vegas isn't the place to have a rest. Every time you sit down somebody starts dealing you cards.'

VC10 Captain at a Harrier squadron party: 'Do you mind if I bring the crew in?'

'Crew? What's that?'

Another Captain in a hotel room in Gander: 'I wish you lot would clear out and let me go to bed.'

'But Captain—this is my room.'

## No 72 Squadron Linebook

**1977**

The sergeants' mess dining hall was plunged into darkness during a power-cut. An intrepid steward emerged from the servery to shout: 'Anybody who wants a candle put their 'and up!'

'What were they saying about force's pay in the *Daily Mail* today?'

'I dunno, I couldn't afford a newspaper.'

**1978**
Briefing a four-ship VIP formation: 'And you've drawn the short straw, Martin—the Station Commander's coming along in your left-hand seat.'

'Oh—I suppose I'd better take a map, then.'

A Captain was speaking to HM Coastguard during an oil tanker incident.

Captain: 'Can we take three BP men out on the next trip?'

HMG: 'No, all runs have to be approved by us and then the Department of Trade and Industry. In fact the VIP run you did yesterday wasn't approved by the Department of Trade and Industry and you shouldn't have done it.'

Captain: 'You do realize that the VIP was the Secretary of State for Trade and Industry!'

**1980**
The squadron had just returned from exercise in Otterburn to find that a case of infectious hepatitis had been reported there and all personnel would therefore have to be innoculated. A squadron leader commented: 'This is the final exercise inject.'

## No 92 Squadron Linebook

**1944**
'The flak was so low I had to go through it on instruments.'

'My personal magnetism corrects all the errors on my compass.'

'There's a new aircraft being delivered to us—it's a Mark XIV, no, a XII—eh, a XI . . . what are we flying now??'

**1945**
'When I was in the desert our squadron did not have a bar in the mess. We decided the best thing would be the tail off a Hun, so next morning I went up and shot down a ME 110 so we could take a drink in the evenings.'

'My operational hours look like the national debt!'

'I've had so many narrow escapes I feel like a fugitive from the law of averages.'

**1949**
Asked the wing span of a Lancaster, a pilot replied confidently '98 feet'. 'But are you sure?' asked another. 'Oh yes, I once taxied one through a 100-foot gap!'

'I knew it was bumpy while flying in formation; I could see my section leader's oxygen mask jumping up and down.'

'You should have seen the sand fall out of my parcel of overseas photographs.'

# No 208 Squadron Linebook

**1984**
Rather portly squadron navigator receiving some severe ribbing from assembled squadron members:

'But at least I will still be warm after two or three hours in the sea.'

'Yeah, but you'll have a harpoon stuck in you.'

**1984**
Duty pilot in ATC asked Controller to ask a returning aircraft for his opinion of the visibility on the final approach:

Controller: 'F37, what is your impression of the vis on finals?'

F37: 'I'm sorry, I don't do impressions.'

**1985**
Pete: 'Rob, do you know you're Mister Vice* tonight?'

Rob: 'Oh no, not again. Why?'

Pete: 'Well, it's either the youngest or the ugliest who has to do it.'

Rob: 'But I'm not the youngest any more!'
[*Dining-In Night Vice-President]

**1986**
A formation came across a fleet of warships and was trying to establish contact:

No 1: 'Tool, this is Hawk. Tool, this is Hawk.'

No reply.

No 2: 'I think they're French.'

No 1: 'Tool, thees eez 'awk. Tool, thees eez 'awk.'

# No 230 Squadron Linebook

Bad Tole (RECCE)—Hotel Diana. Squadron Leader Cogram to George Blackie: 'The Air Force is the only firm that, after twenty-five years, takes your watch away.'

**1979**
Well-known Met Man at night-flying briefing: 'The surface wind is flat, calm . . . but if you want a direction it will be generally north-westerly.'

# No 617 Squadron Linebook

**1983**
At a crew meeting, on being told that the Chief Caterer was to visit the squadron, one was heard to remark: 'Is he one of the Wheels-on-Meals?'

**1984**
During a station exercise, the following radio conversation was recorded:

ATC: '699, just follow the marshallers.'
699: 'But they're going into the coffee bar.'

Pause.

ATC: 'How many sugars do you take?'

**1985**
Pilot 1: 'Hey chaps! The weather's going to be a bit rough on Monday according to the Met man . . .'

Pilot 2: 'I can't believe that—he doesn't even know what the weather did yesterday.'

## Initial Officer Training, RAF College Cranwell Linebook

**Course number 90 A Squadron**
After a particularly bad lead during leadership training, the Flight Commander was debriefing the leader:

Flight Commander: 'Well, Bloggs, let's look at the good things in that exercise.'

Cadet looks surprised.

Flight Commander: 'It did not rain.'

**Course number 94 A Squadron**
Officer Cadet Bloggs giving orders on the march:

'Turn left . . . NOW!'

Officer Cadet Bloggs talking about etiquette: 'Put the wine in the ice bucket? Why not just put the bottle in the bucket?'

**Course number 98 A Squadron**
Conversation at the scramble on the confidence course:

Flight Sergeant Brown: 'Come on, Bloggs, get your leg over.'

Officer Cadet Bloggs: 'Ooh! its sharp up here and I don't have anything in the middle so to speak.'

**Course number 106 A Squadron**
At another debrief:

'Well, what happened to the young lieutenant navigator?'

'Well, sir, as he had made a mess of things, he was given further training so that he could get on better with everybody, feel happier about things in general and get on with his life—but he committed suicide the following day!'

After an oral communications lesson, where he had watched his two-minute talk played back on video, the officer cadet in question was heard to comment: 'Oh my god, I avoid boring people like that in the bar.'

Brown, a serious and somewhat studious cadet, thought hard about the question his flight commander had put to him:

Ma'am: 'Why are women so bad at parking cars?'

Brown: 'Because they have a lack of spatial awareness, ma'am.'

Ma'am: 'No, Brown, it's because for years men have been telling them that's ten inches.'

**Course number 110 A Squadron**

WRAF cadet to flight commander: 'Is it all right if we roll our jacket sleeves up?'

Flight commander: 'What are you wearing underneath?'

WRAF cadet to flight commander: 'Nothing, sir!'

Flight commander in reply: 'Then you may take your jackets off.'

Having been told by the RAF Liaison Officer to uphold the good name of the RAF by dancing with the locals on a French visit, a flight commander looked around for a reasonable target of opportunity.

Having selected a likely-looking young lady, he wandered up and asked in his best French: 'Excusez-moi, mademoiselle, mais voudriez-vous danser avec moi, s'il vous plait?'

The young lady looked at the flight commander, smiled sweetly and said: 'Merci beaucoup, monsieur, mais je ne danse pas avec les hommes, je suis une lesbienne!'

At this point the flight commander decided that tonight was not his night and went to get drunk.

**Course number 107 B Squadron**

During room inspection in week 4:

Flight commander: 'Whatever you do with your uniform, Bloggs, you always look scruffy.'

Bloggs: 'Thank you, sir.'

When talking to the flight commander about the prizes available on graduation:

Officer Cadet Bloggs: 'Is there a cash alternative, sir?'

Flight commander: 'I'm going to have to watch you, Bloggs.'

**Course number 111 B Squadron**
Flight Sergeant Smith to Officer Cadet Prune: 'Why are those two flies mating on your head, Mr Prune? You're not allowed to keep pets.'

RAF Regiment Flight Sergeant to cadets: 'There's so much indecision here that you'll graduate and easily make Air Vice Marshals.'

Officer Cadet Bloggs (WRAF) to Officer Cadet Prune when cleaning weapons:

'Would you like a pull through, Andy?'

'Oh, all right then, but do it inconspicuously, I don't want everyone to know.'

# Jokes

A large tent had been pitched among the foothills of the Aden hinterland, to serve as a temporary mess for army and RAF officers engaged in the protection of the national interest, as then perceived. Very early one morning a solitary figure was taking breakfast—a subaltern of a famous regiment, who had been appointed duty officer for the day and who, by custom, was therefore arrayed in full service dress uniform—including hat. He was reading a three-week-old copy of the *Telegraph*—the latest available. Enter two rather less elegantly attired young RAF pilots, on their return from a dawn reconnaissance sortie—very hot and decidedly less than fresh in their already sodden flying suits. They sat down at the table and duly ordered from the Arab steward the standard aircrew breakfast of bacon and fried eggs, tomato, sausage, baked beans and fried bread. Their cheery morning greeting to their army colleague appeared to have gone unheard, for he was still immersed in his newspaper as he toyed delicately with a bowl of cereal.

In due course came the aircrew breakfast, and one of the young pilots enquired of the back of the newspaper whether the army officer might pass the salt. There was no response—nor, indeed, a flicker of recognition on the slightly louder repeat of the request. However, at the third time of asking, the duty officer wearily laid down his paper and said: 'You RAF chaps obviously don't understand the custom of my regiment. When a chap is sitting in the mess wearing his hat, it means that he wishes neither to speak nor to be spoken to,' and he again disappeared behind the *Telegraph*.

One of the young airmen rose, walked around the table to stand behind the army officer, unlaced a desert flying boot and dropped it carefully into the bowl of cornflakes. Infuriated soldier leaps to his feet, demanding an explanation. 'Oh it's simple, old chap,' said the pilot. 'You chaps obviously don't understand the custom of the Royal Air Force. When a chap drops his flying boot into another chap's cornflakes, it means "Pass the —— salt!"'

Three lifelong friends (amazingly, an admiral, a general and an air marshal) were brought to a sudden and simultaneous end when their aircraft hit a mountain—thus effectively interrupting the rather heated discussion they were having as to the relative importance of the three armed services.

To the slight surprise of one, and the blank astonishment of the others, they found themselves on the glittering pathway to the gates of Heaven, and decided that, as discord must for them be a thing of the past, they had better establish, for their eternal peace of mind, whether a view was held in heaven on such matters as interservice status. St Peter was only too pleased to help.

'Indeed,' said he, 'God has pronounced on that very subject only today.' And to his three newest arrivals he pointed out a wall, fifteen feet high, on which was inscribed, in perfect Gothic script, the words: 'There can be no differentiation as between the relative importance of the three armed services of the British Crown—signed God.'

However, beneath the signature, and in slightly smaller lettering there appeared: 'Air Commodore (retired)'!

'You can't pass this way, sir,' said the AC2. 'I've orders to turn back all motors that come along this road.'

'But I'm the CO!'

'Sorry, sir, I didn't know. My orders are to let no traffic through because of the rotten bridge, but seeing it's you, sir, go right ahead!'

Four elderly men, in a railway carriage, all sitting in opposite corners and saying nothing. After an hour, one stood up and said, 'This is going to be a very dull journey if we don't talk', and said by way of introduction: 'I am a retired Group Captain and have three sons all accountants.' The second said: 'I am a retired Group Captain and have three sons, all solicitors.' The third said: 'I am a retired Group Captain and have three sons, all barristers.' The fourth sat silently in his corner until he was asked, 'How about you', and he answered: 'I am a retired Warrant Officer, unmarried, and I have three sons, all Group Captains!'

An airman on the North-West Frontier of India once found himself short of money. He conceived the brilliant idea of writing to the Almighty for some. His letter ran: 'Dear God, I'm broke, please send me £10.'

In due season, this letter reached the Air Ministry, some say appropriately. Touched by the man's simple faith, a few officers are said to have subscribed the sum of £3, and sent it to him.

Thinking no more of it, what was their amazement, some six months or so later, to receive another letter from the same airman, also addressed to the Almighty. This one ran: 'Dear God, Thank you for the £3. But next time, please don't send it through the Air Ministry, as the so-and-so's have pinched seven.'

The RAF pilot was standing with an American pilot on a USAF base in the UK watching a B-47 jet bomber fully loaded lumbering along and staggering into the air almost at the very end of the runway.

'That looked pretty close,' said the RAF type.

'Yeah,' said the American, 'those machines can only get airborne because the world is round; if it was flat they would never make it.'

The following was overheard on a famine relief operation. Each day they would load the planes with foodstuff or medical supplies and fly them to where they were needed. To assist in loading and unloading the aircraft there was always plenty of local labour, who were cheerful and willing but needed plenty of guidance if the aircraft was to be loaded safely. The sergeant got into the habit of slapping the pile of sacks with his hand to indicate where the next one was to be placed and saying, 'Put it here, Sam', or, 'Let's have that one over here, Willie,' and so on. The locals were always Sam and Willie to him. One day they were being watched by some nuns who had come out from Addis Ababa 'to see for themselves'. After watching with interest for some time and hearing all the Sam this and Willie that, they turned to the Sergeant and said, 'How do you know all their names?'

A fighter escort always flew dangerously close to the DC3s they were supposed to be escorting. One of the DC3 pilots had a pet bear; one day he took it into the cockpit and when the fighters approached he put the bear into the pilot's seat. After one look, they decided to fly further away. Never again did they fly too close. Also, they never mentioned what they had seen. Who would have believed them?

A flight engineer went to station sick quarters for his annual medical. There was a Welsh WAAF medical orderly on duty and she gave him a bottle and told him to give a sample. He went behind the screen and put lager in the bottle and gave it to the orderly.

She tested it and said: 'There's something *terribly* wrong here.' The flight engineer said: 'It seems all right to me,' and proceeded to swallow the lot. The poor orderly fainted.

The young pilot went to an Accountant Officer who was particularly shy of the fact that he had a glass eye. The mercenary request of the pilot was refused: so he leaned across the table, stared at the Accountant Officer and said: 'I know that you have a glass eye.'

The Accountant Officer shivered and whispered: 'Oh, I hoped nobody could tell . . . which one is it?'

The pilot answered: 'The one with the sympathetic expression.'

A squadron leader on retirement decided to become a farmer, rearing poultry and a few crops.

Knowing a friend of his had a small farm, he went to work with him for a week or so to gain experience.

His first job was grading eggs into three sizes, small, medium and large. Three hours later, the farmer returned to see how his friend was getting on, only to find to his dismay that he hadn't even started.

The farmer then decided he had better give him something else to do, so he took him to a field of newly harvested corn and explained that he would like the sheaves of corn stacked neatly in rows, straight lines, one sheaf directly behind the other. An hour later he returned to find to his surprise the work was completed and was perfect.

When asked to explain this the retired officer said: 'The eggs I found difficult as it required a decision, but I really shine when it comes to bull.'

The Station Commander was carrying out his weekly inspection and he included in his itinerary the station barber's shop. In the chair sat an airman receiving a short back and sides. Unfortunately, the use of Service time for such an activity was not popular with the Station Commander.

'Having your haircut in working hours I see,' humphed the CO.

'Yes, sir, it grew in working hours,' replied the airman. The Station Commander was not to be outdone.

'It didn't *all* grow in working hours,' he said.

'No, sir,' responded the airman, 'I'm not having it *all* cut off.'

A train had just arrived at Waterloo and there were no porters around—well, there was a war on. A little old lady with a huge suitcase hailed a passing wing commander.

'I say, porter, could you help me with this?'

The officer decided to humour her and, touching his cap, manfully carried the case to the taxi rank. She thanked him and handed him a half crown.

'Madam,' he protested, 'this is far too much, a shilling would do.'

'Nonsense,' she replied. 'Shillings I give to Pilot Officers.'

A bemused flight lieutenant watched in awe as a hundred helicopters filled the sky over Middle Wallop at 'Army Air 82'.

'It's not natural,' he gasped. 'If God had meant the army to fly he'd have made the sky brown!'

An army unit was flying overseas with Transport Command. As the Air Quartermaster, a flight sergeant, made his way down the aisle, the colonel in charge of the unit called him. 'I say, Staff Sergeant.'

The AQM seemed not to hear and went on to the flight deck.

When he returned, the colonel grabbed him by the sleeve. 'Staff sergeant, I called you just now and you ignored me; you must have heard.'

'Sorry, sir,' he replied, 'I heard you called a Staff Sergeant, I am a Flight Sergeant.'

The colonel flushed angrily. 'Don't be pedantic, man. You've got three stripes and crown. If you were in the army you'd be a Staff Sergeant!'

'Pardon me, sir,' said the AQM. 'If I were in the army I'd be at least a colonel.'

A fighter pilot was bewailing his forthcoming posting to a fighter-bomber squadron; he was particularly incensed about the fact that he would have to fly with a navigator, for he had a full share of the pilots' prejudice against that noble breed.

'Don't be so bigoted, lad,' said a bemedalled colleague. 'Navigators are extremely useful fellows. Indeed, I owe my life to one. When I was on twins in the desert we got shot up and I had to put her down in the bundoo, miles from base. The place was featureless, we had no food, and the sun was merciless. I hadn't even any real idea of where we were, but I'm here today to tell you about it, and that's thanks to my navigator!'

The younger man, impressed, asked, 'What did he do?—guide you back to civilization?'

'No,' said the veteran. 'I ate him.'

An old Avro 504 shed a wheel just as it gained flying speed. Those on the ground believed that neither occupant would appreciate this fact, which could cause a little difficulty on landing. It was therefore decided to send up a second aircraft with a couple of occupants and a spare wheel. The plan was for the second aircraft to formate on the first and for the passenger to indicate by sign language and by showing the wheel that the first aircraft had only one main wheel left. Then the most impossible thing happened. On take-off, the second Avro shed a wheel, without, of course, the pilot or passenger knowing. As briefed, the second aircraft climbed and formated on the first. The passenger duly pointed and waved the wheel above his head from the rear cockpit.

The crew of the first aircraft gave a glance at the second aircraft, minus a wheel, and looked at the passenger waving the wheel above his head. The pilot of the first aircraft then spoke to his passenger over the old-fashioned Gosport tubing, which was the only form of communication in those days. He said: 'That's jolly clever, isn't it? Let's stay up here and see him get it back on again.'

At the height of the desert campaign in World War Two, three khaki-clad RAF officers walked wearily into Shepheards Hotel, Cairo, and ordered cold beer. It was evening, and, as usual in Cairo even during the war, everyone was in full mess dress as the admin wallahs continued to ignore the fighting that was going on in the desert. A brilliantly attired major approached the ill-dressed RAF officers and said: 'I am Major the Hon. —— Assistant Provost Marshal. You chaps are improperly dressed and must leave.'

One of the RAF officers rose slowly to his feet, looked the major straight in the eye and replied: 'I am Group Captain The Earl of Bandon. I outrank you on both counts. Now —— off.'

A party of five trainees was detailed by the Station Warrant Officer. 'Half of you go to the cookhouse and the other half to the coke compound.'

One of the youngsters protested: 'But, sir. There's five of us.' To which the SWO barked: 'Keep your mouth shut when you're talking to me, boy!'

A warrant officer and flight sergeant were arguing the ratio of work to pleasure involved in making love. The warrant officer claimed it was 50–50, but the flight sergeant thought it was 25 per cent work and 75 per cent pleasure. They decided to ask the first airman they met to adjudicate. He ruled: 'It must be 100 per cent pleasure because if there was any work involved neither of you two would be interested.'

A young airman was asked by the Air Officer Commanding the Group what he would like to be.

'An Air Vice-Marshal, sir,' replied the airman.

'Are you crazy?' replied the astonished AOC, to which the airman replied: 'I didn't know that was a necessary qualification, sir.'

A young airman had been courting the CO's daughter for a few years and decided to ask for permission to marry her. The interview went like this:

Airman: 'Sir, I feel that after courting your daughter for three years it is in order for me to ask for her hand in marriage.'

CO: 'My dear fellow, on your pay you couldn't keep her in the way she has been brought up.'

Airman: 'Sir, I have a small private income and I feel we could be very comfortable.'

CO: 'What about a family? Could you support one?'

Airman: 'We don't propose to have any children, sir.'

CO: You mean to tell me you intend to beat the will of God. Impossible, man, impossible.'

Airman: 'Well, sir, we've done all right up to now.'

A retired very senior RAF officer took up rough shooting as a hobby and was alarmed at the high cost of trained dogs. But he was told of a former airman who trained gun dogs and gave good rates to RAF personnel. The season was well under way when contact was made and the only dog left was LAC Bonzo, who would cost £10 for the two weeks. It was explained to the retired officer that each dog was given a rank according to the stage of its training and ability: Bonzo was scarcely out of his basic course. He proved a lovable retriever but a hopeless gun dog. The retired officer, however, was so fond of him that he booked him the following season. He was delighted to discover Bonzo was now a corporal and that the fee was £30. He performed magnificently, so the following season the officer rang again and asked for Corporal Bonzo, but was informed: 'You mean Flight Sergeant Bonzo, who is now £50.'

Flight Sergeant Bonzo proved worth every penny of the new price. He would point, set, quarter and do everything bar load the guns. The retired officer, thanks to Flight Sergeant Bonzo, got the record bag for the season and a full page photograph and report in *Country Life*.

He was so delighted he rang up the kennels and offered to buy Bonzo for £300. Surprisingly enough, he was told he could have him for a tenner.

'Are you talking about Flight Sergeant Bonzo, the dog I've had since he was an LAC? Whatever is the matter?'

Back came the reply: 'Well, he got so good we promoted him to the rank of warrant officer. Now he just sits on his backside all day and barks.'

Pilot to Control: 'What is your cloud cover?'
Control: 'Ten eighths at 100 feet.'
Pilot: 'How can you have ten eighths?'
Control: 'Well, yesterday we had eight eighths and today it's much worse.'

The story is told of a tough, hard-swearing warrant officer rear gunner who flew one night with a squadron leader who was regarded as a 'bible puncher,' a man to whom bad language just was not acceptable. During the flight, the aircraft was jumped by fighters. The rear gunner was swearing like a trooper so the captain spoke to him. Unfortunately, he inadvertently switched his RT to 'transmit' so the complete bombing force heard this conversation:

Captain: 'Don't worry, rear gunner. The Lord is with you.'

Rear Gunner: 'He might be with you up there, but he's bloody well deserted me down here!'

A very young fighter pilot had his aircraft set on fire and when he tried to escape he found the hatch jammed. He then started transmitting to his section, shouting things like: 'I'm trapped. My God, I don't want to die,' and 'Tell my mother I loved her.' Suddenly an Australian voice chipped in with: 'I say, cobber. This is an operation channel. If yer can't die like a gentleman, would yer mind doing it on another frequency?'

Squadron Commander exasperated at hearing another aircrew member had been hurt playing football: 'Do you know, the other day we actually had a squadron crew member unfit for sport due to being hurt in an aeroplane.'

Three uniformed airmen seated in a London cocktail bar were flat broke, but each ordered an expensive drink as if possessed of all the money in the world.

One of them quickly emptied his glass and was about to leave, when the barman said: 'Sir, you've forgotten to pay for your drink.'

The airman spun round in his tracks and said: 'What's that? I did pay for my drink. Didn't I?' he asked the second airman, who also was just about to leave.

'You most certainly did,' agreed his pal. 'You paid the same time as I did. If I were you, I'd report the matter to the management and demand an apology.'

The two airmen then gave the barman a dirty look and left the bar, muttering about his allegation.

The bartender could not believe what had happened. Almost desperately he appealed to the third airman who, with a far-away look in his eyes, was gazing stonily at the bottom of his empty glass.

'Sir,' asked the barman, 'do I look as if I had lost my memory? Your friends who've just left said they'd both paid for their drinks at the same time; but I can't remember receiving a penny from either of them. Tell me, Sir, am I right or am I cuckoo?'

The third airman scowled indignantly at the barman. Then putting down his glass, he drew himself up and said: 'Your mental troubles are none of my concern. Please give me my change and let me get out of this crazy pub.'

When Marshal of the Royal Air Force, Lord Tedder (Deputy Supreme Commander of World War Two), was attending the England–Australia Test Match at the Oval in 1953, he was approached by a small boy for his autograph.

The air marshal thought it well to point out that he was not a cricketer, but the small boy insisted and said, 'I know you've had something to do with the RAF.' Smilingly, Lord Tedder signed his usual signature, 'Tedder'.

'Crumbs!' said the boy to his companion, 'he's just wrote "Teddee". He ain't even got a blumen' surname.'

An RAF education officer was about to give a lecture to some assembled airmen. The sergeant in charge of the proceedings introduced the speaker, saying:

'Mr Leigh-Osborne is now going to give you a talk on Keats, but I don't suppose half you ignorant lot know what a keat is.'

During the last war, a young WAAF was wandering around a London barrage-balloon site looking very miserable. An officer stopped her and asked: 'What's the matter?'

'I've lost a spanner, sir,' she replied dolefully.

'Nonsense,' snorted the officer, 'you can't lose a thing like a spanner.'

'Can't I?' answered the WAAF. 'Ten minutes ago I lost a ruddy balloon as well.'

Old Lady to parachutist: 'I really don't know how you can hang from that silk thing. The suspense must be terrible.'

Parachutist: 'No, Mum; it's when the suspense ain't there that it's terrible.'

'You've got a touch of pneumonia,' said the Medical Officer after examining the air cadet.

'Are you sure, sir?' queried the airman. 'I have known people in civvy street to be told they have pneumonia but then to die of something quite different.'

'You're not in civil life now: you're in the Royal Air Force,' thundered the MO, 'and if you get treated in the Royal Air Force for pneumonia, you die of pneumonia.'

Just after the invasion of Norway, a big German ship laden with munitions came into Bergen. Anxious to get it unloaded as quickly as possible, the Germans went around to all the big employers asking for men to start work next morning at 7 AM. The reply everywhere was: 'There is no work here now for our men, so they have all gone up into the mountains.'

At last the Trades Union Secretary, under strong pressure, gave way. Would the Germans, he inquired, allow him to speak on the radio? Certainly they would. He thereupon broadcast an urgent appeal to all his men to be at Dock X at 7 AM prompt, next morning, to unload munitions from a big German ship.

At a quarter to seven next morning the roads leading to the quay were black with men, their faces turned skyward. At ten minutes to seven, the RAF arrived and sank the ship.

The Station Warrant Officer was always picking on AC Smith when on parade. 'Pay attention, stop moving about, Smith!'

Then one day Smith was on light duties, excused parades and was Room

Orderly. The SWO called the parade to attention and as usual added: 'Stand still, Smith!'

At this, Smith poked his head through the barrack room window and shouted: 'Not me, sir, I'm in here!'

The SWO didn't turn a hair but bellowed, 'Well, the man next to you stand still!'

A Flight Sergeant was addressing a scruffy erk.

'How long have you been in the RAF?'

'Three months, Flight.'

'Are you sure?'

'Yes, Flight.'

'Well, then, how did you manage to get that collar that dirty in only three months?'

Navigator to Pilot: 'Come one degree Port, please.'
Pilot: 'Oh, for Pete's sake, that's impossible, I can't fly to one degree!'
After a couple of minutes silence.
Navigator: 'Four degrees Starboard.'
Pilot: 'Roger.'
One minute silence.
Navigator: 'Come five degrees Port, please.'
Pilot: 'Roger.'
Navigator: 'There you are, easy when you know how.'

In the day room at an RAF Hospital were two disconsolate pilot officers, both in wheelchairs, legs in plaster:
PO 1: 'How'd you get yours broken?'
PO 2: 'Scoring a dramatic last-minute try for the RAF against the army—we won. How'd you get yours?'
PO 1: 'Dining-in Night. Quietly drinking on the Ante-Room mantelpiece but fell off. Would have been all right but some drunken fool ran over me on a motor-bike.'

It was Friday and the flight sergeant was a bit late in getting away to catch the bus, to catch the train, to get him home for the weekend. He rushed madly into the Sergeants' Mess, rapidly changed into civilian clothes, grabbed his weekend case and, slapping his trilby on his head, ran towards the bus stop. Coming along in the opposite direction was the Station Commander, leisurely strolling towards his quarter. The flight sergeant slowed to a rapid walk and, forgetting that he was in 'civvies', gave the Station Commander an extremely smart salute—too late he realized his error! With a slight smile, the Station Commander politely raised his uniform cap and passed on.

A group of young servicemen were to be assessed as Potential Officer Material. It was a cold, windy day and beginning to rain. The Assessing Officer, slightly hungover, wanting a coffee and wishing to complete the assessment as quickly as possible, addressed the candidates outside the Reception hut.

'Right, Gentlemen,' he stated, 'one of you is to be selected as Potential Officer Material. Time is short and I haven't got all day, so decide amongst yourselves who is the one most suited for selection and report to me in the Hut.' (Thinks—'I'll have time for a coffee.')

The Assessing Officer turned and went into the hut and, as he sat down at his desk, was confronted by one of the candidates. Hiding his annoyance he said.

'So, young man, what makes you think that you are most suited for selection?'

'Well, sir,' says the young hopeful, shyly, 'I'm not outside getting soaked!'

Driving with an Ace night-fighter pilot in the blackout one night, we were rather shaken by his tendency to hug the kerb and peer into the mirror.

We looked round for the cause of his apprehension, and saw that we were being followed at a slow pace by something showing a small light. Soon an old farm-hand pedalled past on a bicycle.

'That's better,' said the Ace, heaving a sigh of relief. 'I just can't *bear* anything on my tail.'

A squadron of the RAF Regiment advancing through the desert was running short of food and water. After a further forage of ten or eleven days, the squadron was beginning to show signs of thirst. ('Even the Regiment,' writes our informant, 'cannot go without water for an indefinite period.')

On the fifteenth day, they arrived at a water-hole 'with their tongues hanging out', whereupon the Squadron Commander threw his hands in the air and cried: 'Water, water, thank heaven! Now we can get our equipment blancoed!'

The newly-qualified pilot took his batman up for the first time, and proceeded to twist, loop, dive, and do all the fancy tricks known, during which his passenger just gasped and held on for dear life.

After one particularly hair-raising stunt, the airman turned and shouted: 'I bet fifty per cent of those down there thought we were going to crash.'

'Yes, sir,' gulped the batman, 'and fifty per cent up here thought so, too!'

A trolley, loaded with bombs on which some Armoury types had chalked various greetings to the enemy, trundled up to a Stirling. A corporal standing at the bomb doors read off the various inscriptions: 'Hold this one,' 'Love to Adolf,' 'One back from Poplar', and so on. But he couldn't make head or tail of one.

'Shockin' 'andwritin',' he said, aggrieved. 'If I can't read it, I'm sure them Jerries can't.'

Sergeant, drilling air recruits: 'Today, we are 'aving a practice parachute descent. Remember, when yer jumps from the h'aeroplane, count ten, then pull the cord, an' yer gently floats to the ground like a bird. An' if, by any chance, yer parachute don't open, bring it back ter me an' I'll give yer another!'

A few officers, when giving a pre-retirement farewell speech at a dining-out, will seize the opportunity presented by the occasion to regale their captive audiences with an exceedingly long account of their, often modest, careers.

On one such occasion, the speaker, spurred by a certain bitterness, was reducing the audience to total numbness. In the candle-lit gloom, a young officer, armed with an empty wine bottle, was detailed to crawl along the floor until he was in the right position to deal the speaker a silencing blow.

At the critical moment, overcome with excitement, the assailant missed his target: the bottle slewed smack on to the head of the Station Commander.

As the Station Commander groaned and slumped forward, he managed to gasp, 'Hit me again. I can still hear the b—'

A senior officer and his wife at RAF North Cotes decided to give the once-over to a young RAF Binbrook flying officer who had been dating their daughter for some weeks, so they invited him to Sunday afternoon tea. Despite being given a friendly welcome at the appointed time, the young man proved to be extremely nervous. Before long, the conversation faltered into a strained silence.

Making a desperate effort, the young man, inspired by the reputation of RAF North Cotes for bracing sea breezes, turned to his hostess and said hesitantly, 'I believe you suffer very badly from wind.'

Without batting an eyelid, she smiled sweetly at him and replied, 'Not me, my dear, my husband.'

During a tri-service discussion in the NAAFI one night about officers and their usefulness or otherwise, a soldier said: 'In the army our officers lead us into battle.'

A sailor said: 'Oh, on board ship we have to live with the beggars all the time and there's no escape.'

An airman said: 'It's all right for us in the RAF because what we do with our officers is to strap them into an aircraft, point them towards the war zone and wave them bye bye. So they don't cause us any problems.'

The University Air Squadron solo student had left part of his Bulldog T.1 aircraft just beyond the runway threshold, done a 180 degree past the hangar line, and created a Category 5 mess in the grass. He emerged pale but unscathed.

Asked by an observer whether the pilot had been injured, the Contractor's Aircraft Engineering Manager replied: 'No, they wouldn't let me near the little bugger!!'

A party of journalists assembled on the apron for briefing by the navigator, prior to a photo-reconnaissance flight. Watching the pilot carry out some pre-flight checks, a young reporter asked why he was banging the panels on the aircraft. Came the laconic reply, 'He's looking for the door.'

During a lecture on Nuclear, Biological and Chemical (NBC) ground defence, an NCO instructor was revising aspects of NBC first aid.

'What would you do,' he asked the class, 'if you saw someone running down the road in his NBC kit, with no respirator on, foaming at the mouth, acting incoherently and waving his rifle around like a maniac?'

Some bright spark in the class answered, 'Salute him.'

On a quiet Sunday evening, a very young and junior officer entered the bar in his mess to find only one other person there, an elderly, well-dressed, distinguished-looking gentleman whom he did not know. With youthful enthusiasm, the youngster introduced himself and explained that he had just heard a tremendously good new joke about navigators and was bursting to tell someone.

The elderly gentleman responded very coolly, but, despite his displayed indifference, was quite unable to put off the young pilot. In some desperation, the distinguished visitor finally raised his voice and successfully stopped the youngster, who was into the first few words of his new joke: 'Before you go any further, young man, you would wish to know that I am a serving air marshal and, moreover, that I am a navigator.'

Without hesitation, and still bubbling with irrepressible enthusiasm to tell his joke, the young pilot responded: 'Oh, OK, sir, I'll tell it *very* slowly,' and continued!

A squadron leader was taking over a rather difficult appointment from another. At the end of the handover, the out-going squadron leader said, 'You are bound to get problems and when you do, open these three envelopes as need be.

After only two months a crisis arose and the new boy opened envelope No 1. On a card inside it said, 'Blame your predecessor.' This he did and just scraped by.

A further three months and another crushing problem—so to envelope No 2. 'Say you're reorganizing' it advised. He did so but senior management was noticeably displeased!

Only six months later he was confronted by another insoluble dilemma. Feverishly he opened the last envelope—the note inside read: 'Prepare three envelopes.'

A Royal Air Force Air Sea Rescue helicopter was on a routine training exercise over the Outer Hebrides when it developed engine trouble. The young flying officer just managed to land on the sandstrip that serves as the airport for the island of Barra. 'Excuse me,' he said to an old lady who was digging for cockles. 'Is there a mechanic on the island?' She thought hard, then slowly shook her head. 'No,' she said. 'On Barra we are mostly MacNiels.'

At a critical stage of the war, the Chief of the Air Staff and his two colleagues had spent half an hour with Churchill pleading the cause of Bomber Command. As they left, Lord Hankey said:

'There go three men with but a single thought.'

'If that,' growled Churchill.

# Miscellany

## What The Squadron Leader Really Means

**Command and staff jottings**

| | |
|---|---|
| Have you any comments? | What the hell's this about? |
| Please speak | I can't read your rotten writing. |
| Referred for remarks | You're junior to me, you do it. |
| Concur generally | I haven't read it so won't commit myself. |
| I hear what you say | I'm not listening. |
| In spite of what you say | I'm not listening. |
| Your comments noted | I'm not listening. |
| Under consideration | I have lost the file. |
| It is my considered opinion | I have heard my staff say. |
| A growing body of opinion | I agree with my staff. |
| Opinion is widely held | So does AOC. |
| It can be said without fear of contradiction | I am AOC. |

**Examiner's Comments**

| | |
|---|---|
| Shows originality | Non-standard techniques. |
| Says what he thinks | Non-standard phraseology. |
| His experience shows | Uses out-of-date techniques. |
| Firm management | He's a bully. |
| He shows willing | Can't do it. |
| He tries hard | Can't do it. |
| Has good theoretical knowledge | Can't do it. |

**Annual Confidential Reports**

| | |
|---|---|
| Shows exceptional ability | He repairs my car. |
| Career-minded | He agrees with me. |
| Has sound judgement | He agrees with me. |
| He quickly recognizes good ideas | He agrees with me. |
| Has long experience | About time the old fool retired. |
| He has firm opinions | Stubborn. |
| He works long hours | Can't cope. |
| Has the ability to motivate others | He's a bully. |
| In close touch with his airmen | I saw him talk to one. |

He has a great organizing ability ..................... That was a great party.
Creative thinker ................................................ He has crazy ideas.
Always impeccably dressed .............................. He's a smarmy poof.
Active socially ............................................... He drinks like a fish.
His wife supports him socially .......................... She drinks like a fish.
He drinks wisely ........................................... He buys me one too.
Expresses his opinions confidently .................... He seeks my opinion.
His opinions are supported by facts ............................. Troublemaker.

## What Are Waafs?

A WAAF is neither a bit of stuff, a bag of tricks, a fisher of men, a lady of leisure, a blessed Madonna, a Dresden ornament, a useful kitchen crock, an intriguing Circe, a scheming Delilah, a deceptive Eve, or a paragon of virtue. Nor is she that product of Air Ministry, a cross between a tomboy, a Gremlin, known as an Air-woman. She is a natural woman; and therefore she is an unknown quantity composed of all those adverse elements in greater or lesser degree, and skilfully blended by the Great Creator to make up one unique *objet d'art*.

This fact should be clearly understood by every natural man. Before he begins to evince interest in a natural woman he should first examine the piece disinterestedly, and discover which of the aforesaid elements is most apparent in her make up. If he is not a sound judge of natural women he should consult some connoisseur in the art before he attempts to collect the curios around him. Otherwise he may find that his interest in women has proved an expensive and unprofitable hobby.

He will find it very difficult to discover a natural man who is a sound judge of a natural woman (even connoisseurs are liable to make bad deductions). He should therefore, not spend all his youth in male company searching for this rare creature, otherwise he may find himself on the shelf, without having acquired any knowledge of women.

He should, as soon as he is old enough to notice them, spend all this spare time in feminine company searching for a natural woman. He will then, by trial, error, and experience, which is the only reliable method, acquire enough knowledge of women to show him how impossible it is for a mere male to become a sound judge.

He may at the same time, happen upon the unique *objet d'art* which he seeks to ornament his bedside table, namely his ideal woman. If he is a bold bidder and prepared to gamble his entire life, fortune and career on the throw, he may win her against strong opposition from his friends. His happiness will then be assured and he will become successful and respected.

IF HE IS NOT A BOLD BIDDER HE DOES NOT DESERVE TO WIN EITHER A NATURAL WOMAN, A BEDSIDE ORNAMENT, A USEFUL KITCHEN CROCK, SUCCESS IN THIS WORLD, OR SATISFACTION IN THE NEXT.

*The Tropic Times*, 1944

# Solicitations

To:

A. C. W. Winter, O. B. E.,
Officer Commanding, R. A. F. Depot,
Karachi.

Sir,

Your photo in the Times of India dated the 23rd instant encouraged me to approach you for the fullfillment of my ambition of getting any service in Royal Air Force.

As regards for my qualifications it is sufficient to say that I can please my superiors in every respects.

Awaiting for your kind and favourable consideration.

Thanking you in anticipation.

I beg to remain,
sir,
Your most obedient servant,
(Sgd) B. K. L.

Indore.
28th Nov. 1929.

*Answer to above*:

Dear Sir,

It is regretted that at present no vacancies exist at this Depot.

(Sgd) W. H. O'L.

*Answer to above*:

To: The Officer Commanding,
Aircraft Depot, R. A. F., Karachi.

Sir,

Almighty has favoured on me, for, my application has drawn your kind attention and as per yours of the 7th instant bearing the No. A/109/a created a stray hope in me that whenever any vacancy occurs under your kind control my humble request for serving would be dealt with seniority.

For the time being your a bit of little more favour, for allowing me to under go the unpaid candidateship either in mechanic or Postal Branch, would make up me rather easier to prove myself to be able hand for my future undertakings.

Sir, Please note that I being all alone in this hemisphere wanted to passaway up above the world so high as not to render the earthen affairs.

Shortly to say you is this that I am grasping in darkness for my futures hence I am demanding the favourable, but unavoidable death than—heaps of wealth.

Considering this natural right demand I hope this would tell upon any concious and requesting you to treat me not as a trafelling mere service demanding factor.

I think it is sufficient to penant the poor interiors of my heart gusshing out for an Administrative.

Thanks for your balance of mind.

Awaiting for your kind action to this.

I am to remain,
Ever yours humble,
(Sgd) B. L. K.

Indore.
Dated the 19th Dec. 1929.

Karachi, 10th April, 31.

To:- The Chief Fly Officer i/c I.T.S.
Aircraft Depot, R. A. F.
Drigh Road, Karachi.

Respected Sir,

I most respectfully beg to state that I am heartily wishing to join military services. So I request your kind honour to kindly grant me some suitable job, I am fit for; or at the least kindly take me as apprentice in your Motor work shop or the Airoplane repairing work shop.

As regards my qualifications, I have studied up to matriculation in the Bombay University; and possess practical knowledge of Surveying and drawing i.e. I am a drafts man and as Surveyor as well.

Moreover I beg to state that I am a real artizen at Wood work. So I specially beg to give to your notice that I am a experienced carpenter and a little experted painter as well, and I am a Polish-man too.

I hope you shall be also glad to know that I am a grown up boy at the young age of 25 years, possessing good health. So faithing in our God I am to say that I will be able to face any trouble that might occurs in my service course.

I hope you shall be good enough to give me a start. For which act of your Holiness I shall be highly obliged and shall pray for your long life and prosperity.

I beg to remain
Sir
Your most obedient Servant
(Sgd) M. A. R.

## Letter Home

Same 'ole
September, 1946.

Dere Mums;

This is 'Erb talking to yer from Rangoon in Burma, as I thought as 'ow yer mite like to 'ave a bit a gossip ter tell Aunt Flo over yer Guinness at the local on Saterday nite.

Well, 'Taint 'arf reel owt 'ere. Theres Temples and wot they calls Pagodas, witch is sposed to be bootiful, but yer 'as ter trapse around in yer bare feet, on an 'ot marble floor, an, oh Ma, the stink, an things yer 'as ter tread in. Then theres the natives. The men wears a silk skirt rite dahn ter their ankles, an as fer the dames, they smokes fat cigars. They sleeps on the road, and wot do yer think, they all spits.

Corse, we British keeps to ourselfs, an the camp reely is a loverly place wen yer gets yewsed to it. Its a bit 'ard sumtimes to understand the R. A. F. language, specially the officers, oo ses things is Wizard, an Bang on. That's daft aint it, cos you and me's got brains Ma, an we noes that a Wizard is one of them blokes in a big 'at, wot comes ter the Ipp. on Saterdays an makes things vamoosh. The men aint much better either, cos they sometimes talks abaht a shower, an they don't mean rain at all, an a sprogg is wot they calls a new officer we got.

We as some special grub 'ere too, called M & V but I aint allahd ter tell yer jus wot it tastes likes cos, that would be bad for morals or summat like that, but won day I eres a guy in the cookhouse, say as ow it was somthink ter do wiv camels. Still we 'as an Orficer cum rownd ter see if we is all 'appy at meals every daiy an won day it was a screem, cos one bloke ses ee wasn't, an e's bin doin extra dooties ever since. Aint it the dogs dinner. The Orficer wos a bit La-di-da, an ee wore 'is wings under is nose, an sed wot at the end of everythink, so's we dunno if ee was asking us or tellin us.

There's sum rum complaints ere too, but the M. O. allus gives us a big pill as ses its Dissenterry. Funny thing is yer gets this in sum special ouses in the town, but theys put them owt of bahnds nah. Ere Ma, wot do yer think— don't tell Aunt Flo this, but they puts stuff in yer tea, though we don't no sactly wot for, cept that one bright spark ses it was cos we was young and full of the joys of spring.

We gets pitchers on the camp too, but the seets is 'ard, an makes yer bum a bit num Mum through the big film. Wen Dotty Lamoor comes on all the blokes wistles and fijits 'an shouts things, which I 'spose is cos its so 'ot. Anyway we tells 'em they is rahnd the bend, an then they gets on wiv there beer. We wos in tents, but nar that the eavy rain as stopped, weve moved into sum noo smashin' 'uts, but they leaks too, which is just ter keep us tuff.

'Ope things is O.K. wiv you Ma, but I guess you'll allus be O.K. wile theres a drop a Muvvers ruin goin. I'll buy yer a bigg un, aht of all my War Gratooities wen I get's ome. It won't be long nah wiv all this speed up in Demob as we Group 50 blokes 'opes ter be aht within the next year.

I'll drop a few more lines soon, opin this finds yer as it leaves me at present, 'ot but 'appy.

Yore devoted son,
Erb.

P.S. Don't let young 'Arry were aht my best bit of noo trasers.

D. E. Waller,
*Transcript*, The Magazine of No. 26 PTC Rangoon, September 1946

# The Hurricane and the Sardine

**The repair and recovery of a Hawker Hurricane from Liberia in 1941 using a sardine can as a condenser**

Large cumulus clouds collected and things looked ominous from time to time but the rain held off. Within two or three days the Hurricane was standing on its wheels with the undercarriage down and locked. The propeller had arrived and our native friends from the village carried it in its dismantled state on their heads to the site. The radiator was full of sand and we sat underneath with bamboo slivers and poked it out until the matrix was clear. Everything was checked and appeared to be in order. There was very little petrol in the tanks. We half filled two drums at Roberts Field so that they could be floated ashore and rolled to the site. Talk about 'Saunders of the River'! You could hear our friends rolling the barrels through the bush for miles. Every evening Jones and I had a pay parade. Those carrying light loads got 3*d.* and the heavy load carriers got 6*d.* We paid them in English money so that I have no idea of what use they made of it—possibly earrings! In any case everyone appeared to be satisfied.

Guns, ammunition and everything else that was weighty and could be removed was removed. At last the great moment arrived to start the engine. It wouldn't. The ignition was checked and the spark was found to be very weak. It was lunchtime and we sat down to eat. Our rations included some sardines and some chocolate. The chocolate was wrapped in waxed paper. After some discussion it was the general view that as the booster coil was situated at the bottom of the engine bay its condenser had probably been lying in water and was rendered unserviceable.

It was not the sort of spare part that was readily available and in any case it might take several days to get a replacement and each day we could expect rain. Red McKenny suggested that we should make a condenser out of the sardine cans using the waxed chocolate paper as a dielectric. We all sat round cutting the cans into strips. Red assembled the finished product, wrapped it round with some insulation tape and after Jones had attached it to the booster coil, all was ready for another try to start the engine. Jones got into the cockpit, settled himself down, pressed the starter button choof, choof, two compressions and a cloud of smoke and there we stood watching the engine running as sweet as a nut. When he had given the engine time to warm up, Jones opened the throttle and the engine roared away . . .

As soon as the others arrived by boat the story of the sardine can condenser made the rounds and a splendid evening of ballyhoo ensued. Red McKenny was the magician of the hour and the pair of us enjoyed free drinks and much leg pulling until late into the night.

The next morning, leaving Jones and the rest of the party to change the engine for a new one to be sent from Takoradi, I returned to Air Headquarters. 'So you managed to salvage the Hurricane,' said the AOC as I entered his office. 'Yes, sir.' I told him the story of the sardine can condenser and the tremendous help that McKenny had been to us. 'Good,' he said, and I then saluted and returned to my veranda.

# Air-Action

*As told in the Bible*

In the Bible may be found many references to man's aspirations to flight, but perhaps you may not know that a description is also given of 'air-action'.

A state of peace exists in a mandated territory when suddenly one of the tribes commits an act of war, for 'He hath put forth his hands against such as be at peace with him: he hath broken his covenant. The words of his mouth were smoother than butter, but war was in his heart: his words were softer than oil, yet were they drawn swords.' (*Ps.* LV, 20, 21.) The Political Officer orders the Air Officer Commanding to drop a warning ordering the tribe to come into headquarters, failing this, within forty-eight hours they would be bombed: and telling them that 'For every battle of the warrior is with confused noise, and garments rolled in blood; but this shall be with burning and fuel of fire.' (*Is.* IX, 5.) But this advice is ignored. The Political Officer then sends a wireless telegraphic message to the Air Officer commanding 'Prepare war: stir up the mighty men: let all the men of war draw near, let them come up.' (*Joel* III, 9.) 'When thou comest nigh unto a city to fight against it, then proclaim peace unto it. And it shall be, if it make thee answer of peace and open unto thee, then it shall be, that all the people that is found therein shall be tributaries unto thee. And if it will make no peace with thee, but will make war against thee, then thou shalt besiege it.' (*Deut.* XX. 10, 11, 12.) The Air Officer commanding then orders the Squadron Commander to 'Prepare for war against her and let us go up at noon.' (*Jer.* VI, 4.) The latter mutters 'I will execute vengeance in anger and fury upon the heathen such as they have not heard.' (*Mic.* V, 15.)

The 'operation orders' are issued—'From twenty years old and upward: all that are able to go forth to war.' (*Num.* I, 3.) The married officers were excused for 'When a man hath taken a new wife, he shall not go out to war, neither shall he be charged with any business: but he shall be free at home one year, and shall cheer up his wife which he hath taken.' (*Deut.* XXIV, 5.) The Squadron Commander, a mighty man for, 'He rode upon a cherub and did fly. He was seen upon the wings of the wind' (*II Sam.* XXII, 11), gathers the pilots together and impresses upon them the necessity of keeping in formation for 'Two are better than one; because they have a good reward for their labour. For if they fall, the one will lift up his fellow: but woe to him that is alone when he falleth: for he hath not another to help him up.' (*Eccles.* IV, 9, 10.) The squadron takes off 'With wings as eagles' (*Is.* XL, 31), but one luckless pilot stops his engine and is told by his Commanding Officer, 'Shall your brethren go to war and shall ye sit here?' (*Num.* XXXII, 6.)

The movements of the squadron are wirelessly controlled, 'For a bird of the air shall carry the voice, and that which hath wings shall tell the matter.' (*Eccles.* X, 20.) The tribe is sighted. Quick comes the order 'Scatter thou the people that delight in war.' (*Ps.* LXVIII, 30.) The bombs are released and 'They beat down the cities, and on every good piece of land cast every man his stone, and filled it; and they stopped all the wells of water, and felled all the good trees' (*II Kings* III, 25), with the result that the recalcitrant tribe 'bowed down their heads, and made obeisance.' (*Gen.* XLIII, 28.) The squadron is ordered back, and the Air Officer Commanding, well pleased, said to the officers on their return, that every man should sit 'under his vine and his fig tree' (*Micah* IV, 4) and be at rest.

C.F.S.G.

*From: the Menu for the Eleventh Annual Reunion Dinner of those officers who served at Great Yarmouth from 1913 to 1920, held at the Café Royal on 25 October 1930.*

# Happy Landing

Johnson felt his aircraft shudder as cannon shells ripped into the fuselage. A stream of oil and glycol belched past his eyes, spattering the cockpit sides, as 'O for Orange' dipped earthwards in its dive of destruction. Johnson felt himself drifting into the misty half world of the sub-conscious.

He struggled frantically to ward off the insidious power that sapped his mind, and drew the energy from his clawing arms, and held him rooted to his seat. The death scream of the shattered engine was like the mocking laughter of the gods in Johnson's tortured ears.

Gently he subsided into the vague world of retrospect. Slowly out of the mists appeared Betty, clad in the dress she had been wearing at the last dance they had been to before he came off leave. It was a filmy creation, with a satiny touch as they danced, the intriguing light was still in her eyes, the smell of her hair, like an apple orchard after an April shower, the smooth movement of bodies in unison to a Gypsy Orchestra.

Through the draperied mists that drifted before his eyes he watched her, lived again the touch of hands in crowded restaurants, the clash of eyes above the heads of a crowd.

Slowly the mists began to disappear, as though drawn away and evaporated by some invisible presence.

Johnson's staring red veined eyeballs hovered between reality and oblivion, he raved 'Good God, it can't happen like this, there's so much to live for.' There was Betty, smiling in front of him. A sound like the croak of a bullfrog came from his throat, the misty vaporous figure of Betty was disappearing, gradually disintegrating into thin air.

He felt the final touch of her hand on his head as she disappeared, and then he awoke to reality—raving.

There was still the touch of a hand on his forehead, the smell of ether was in the air, a trim white dressed figure stood by his side. She nodded her head disprovingly. 'These tonsilitis cases are always the worst,' she said.

Sergeant G. A. Elliman,
Squadron Newsletter *Airmen Only*, May 1945

# Letters From Home

The following are true extracts of letters from wives and sweethearts that were written to Prisoners of War in Germany during World War Two. The prisoners were airmen, mainly from Bomber Command.

'I was so glad you were shot down before flying became dangerous.'

'Darling, in your May letter you asked for slippers, what colour would you like?'

'I wrote to you last week, but nothing came of it, so here we are again!'

'The words after lousy when describing your new camp were obliterated!'

'Darling, I hope you are behaving yourself at the dances and not drinking too much.'

'How are your Father and Mother now? I haven't seen them lately!'

'Have you see the latest film "Stage Door Canteen"?'

'Joe is in Stalag VIIb, I hope you will pop over and see him!'

'Are the German girls good dancers?'

'I am going down to Kent in a few days, do you mind? Write and let me know.'

'I sent off your personal parcel this Friday, you should get it next Thursday. I put in some lovely mince pies but the Red Cross sent them back.'

'Darling, I've just had a baby, but don't worry, the American officer is sending you cigs every week.'

## Extract from Station Routine orders at RAF Dishforth, 1961:

'Wednesday 5th June there will be a domestic evening. The airmen will wash the windows as well as the airwomen.'

## The Beverley—Another Thoroughbred

Once upon a time a famous aircraft designer saw a Dutch barn blow past in a gale. At that moment the basic idea of the Beverley was born.

The original design of the machine was intended to fulfil single-seat fighter specifications, but as it was found that full power was required to taxi the aircraft forward at a slow walking pace, another engine was added. The resulting increase in all up weight necessitated the addition of two more engines to enable it to move at all.

By this time the general dimensions had increased more than somewhat, and work was often delayed for several days at a time while the aircraft was utilized by the airport manager as a spare hangar for visiting aircraft.

This state of affairs continued for so long that by the time the prototype was ready for flight, all other types of aircraft were jet-powered. This rather embarrassed the designer who, not wishing to appear behind the times, therefore had the propellers placed much higher than he had originally intended, in the hope that they would not be noticed. (The production manager raised the roof.) This entailed raising the mainplane and the fuselage sides, which accounts for the immense height of the machine.

As no adequate runway was available, the undercarriage was adapted to take locomotive wheels, and its first take-off was from both tracks of the Brough–Hull railway. It became airborne by the time it reached the passenger station at Beverley—hence the name. A conversion kit is still available for this purpose. When the aircraft is in this role, the flight deck must at all times be referred to as the driver's cab, and the VHF radio should be re-crystallized to include the frequencies of Crewe signal box, and the head office of the National Union of Railwaymen.

Spinning of the aircraft is not recommended as the torque reaction involved causes the earth to rotate in the opposite direction to the spin, to the accompaniment of terse notes from the Greenwich Observatory.

The aircraft is very versatile and many be employed in many roles, particularly those which *do not* include flying or movement of any kind. It is extremely amenable to modification; for example, wind tunnel tests show that the wings could be placed at the bottom, and the wheels at the top without any appreciable drop in performance.

All in all, the Beverley is an ideal aircraft for a civilian enthusiast, with a million pounds, a private oil well, and a complete and utter abhorrence of flying.

## Extract Taken from the Minutes of the Messing Committee Meeting at RAF Calshot, *circa* 1954

'A.C. Sturgess complained that there were cockroaches in the soup.

Flt. Sgt. Tweedy stated that these were not cockroaches but beetles and the matter was closed.'

## King's Regulations

In 1918 the index of King's Regulations for the RAF suggests that a joker was at work:

Abroad, insane officer sent home from
Lunatic women, from abroad, disposal of
Mantel-pieces, draping of, forbidden
Married roll, wife of airman on, deprived of
benefits through misconduct

By 1924, an altogether richer year, the index to KRs contained these items:

Aeroplanes, to give way to balloons and airships
Air Ministry, officers visiting to wear field boots if of rank of squadron-leader or above
Aircraft, dogs carried in, forbidden
Airmen, boys not to foregather with other, when off duty
Airmen, keys of safes or chests, may not be entrusted with
Airships, to give way to balloons
Artificial eyes, provision of
Balloons, airships out of control, classed as

Boys, must write home every week
Civil Power, airman sentenced to death by, service gratuity not issuable
Combination suits, when and how worn
Dope, medical inspection of airmen employed in doping rooms
Dope, special meals for dopers
Mess, officers', liveries for waiters and butlers at
Pilots, breeding stocks, to avoid flying low over
Puttees, airmen unable to wear, procedure
Regulations, participation in public discussion regarding forbidden
Sedition, preached in church, action
White flag, offence to display, how tried

# Rank

**Air Marshal**
Can leap tall buildings with a single bound
More powerful than a steam train
Faster than a speeding bullet
Walks on water and
Gives policy to God

**Air Commodore**
Can leap tall buildings with a running start
More powerful than a diesel engine
Just as fast as a speeding bullet
Walks on water if sea is calm
Discusses policy with God

**Group Captain**
Leaps short buildings with a single bound
More powerful than tank engines
Can occasionally keep up with speeding bullet
Walks on water in small lakes
Talks with God

**Wing Commander**
Leaps short buildings with a running start
Is almost as powerful as a tank engine
Is able to avoid a speeding bullet
Walks on water in indoor swimming pools
Talks to God if special request granted

**Squadron Leader**
Can just clear a small hut
Loses tug of war with tank engine
Can fire a speeding bullet
Swims well
Is occasionally addressed by God

**Flight Lieutenant**
Demolishes chimney when leaping small huts
Is run over by steam trains
Can handle a gun
Dog paddles adequately
Talks to animals

**Flying Officer**
Runs into buildings
Recognises steam trains two times out of three
Is not issued with guns
Can stay afloat with Mae West
Talks to walls

**Pilot officer**
Falls over doorsteps
Says I see no trains
Wets himself with water pistol
Stays on dry land
Mumbles to himself

**Warrant Officer**
Lifts tall buildings and walks under them
Kicks steam trains off the tracks
Catches bullets in his teeth
Freezes water with a single glance
Because he is God

# RAF to ROF

Message to Royal Ordnance Factories from Air Marshal A. T. Harris CBE OBE AFC, Commander-in-Chief, Bomber Command.

'Bombs you have made have been dropped in all Bomber Command's recent attacks on Western Germany, on the Baltic Port of Lubeck, and on the great French factories which worked for Hitler.

'If you have seen the photographs of the damage we have lately done in Germany and France you will know that your bombs have hit the enemy hard, keep at it, and we shall keep at it too.

'Between us we're the only people in this country to keep up an export trade to Germany; we mustn't neglect our duty to our customers.'

# Square Bashing

Overheard on the Parade Ground

'When I was a little boy I had some lead soldiers and I cried when I lost them. Mommy said, "Don't cry, one of these days you will find them again." And I bloody well have!!'

'Head up, shoulders back, fingers curled, thumbs on top, dig your heels in, thumbs in line with the seam of your trousers, chest out, stomach in, look your own height, stand still, **AS YOU WERE**!!'

'When I sez fix . . . wait for it . . . when I sez fix . . . yer don't fix. But when I sez BAYNITS! . . . yer wips 'em out and wops 'em on an' lets 'em glitter in the sun.'

## 'BBB'

During his visits to Bomber Command stations, Air Marshal 'Bomber' Harris was frequently reported as saying: 'We are all here to win the war! I don't want to see the stones whitewashed, the broom handles cleaned or the window brasses polished. Remember BULLSHIT BAFFLES BRAINS!'

## Letter to *The Times*, 1941

'Vere de Vere—Percy Albert, Flight Lieutenant, RAF VR, wishes to notify all his friends of his change of address from Eaton Square to ? Oflag, Germany.'

## RAF Cosford, 1940

ORDERS FOR FIRE PICKET—INCENDIARY BOMBS

**1.** The Stirrup Pump is the best defence against such devices:

- **a.** No. 1 (The Corporal) will point his jet at the bomb.
- **b.** No. 2 will pump vigorously with up and down strokes.
- **c.** No. 3 will pass water.

**2.** Stirrup Pumps not being available, the crew should use sandbags:

- **a.** No. 1 will approach the bomb with the bag held vertically at arms length in front of his body in case it explodes.
- **b.** In the absence of sandbags, the NCO I/C is to use his head.

## All Gloves Are Grey in the Night

From the far end of the kitchen floated the gentle voice of she who must be obeyed. 'I want you to clear the snow from the garden path right away, you will need your gloves.' By that she meant my old leather flying gloves, it so happens that they are the only ones I have, it depresses me to be reminded of all the jolly good gloves of mine which have inexcusably been carelessly lost without trace. My old flying gloves are the only ones I have never been able to lose.

It was a cold wintry day a long time ago when I was first marched to a Royal Air Force Equipment Section to be given a full scale of the approved pre-war regulation flying clothing, there was a lot of it and I carefully scrutinised each item, eventually I screwed up enough courage to complain. 'These are odd gloves, one is light brown and the other is dark brown.' The type of persons with whom I get into arguments always seem to be much bigger men, barrel chested, hairy armed and pugnacious, the equipment assistant was no exception.

I flinched a little as he leaned over the counter in a menacing manner and replied. 'One is left hand, one is right hand, two gloves both the correct size make a pair. The orders are to supply you with a pair of gloves which is exactly what I am doing. Nowhere in the schedule is there any mention of colour.' I protested further. 'They look daft, everybody will notice them wherever I go.' But it was in vain and he remained adamant. For some considerable time I cherished a hope that I would encounter the unfortunate individual who had accepted the other mismatched pair but I never did and I have wondered what his fate was.

Each glove carried an internal label and even the labels are dissimilar, one boldly announces that it is a 'Right Outer' Type 'D', Garment No. W8386 Size 9 No. 10440, Ref 22C/770 and displays the world famous stamp of the Broad Arrow to warn that it is Government Property. The other label is more flattering in a subtle way, it does not bother to say that it is a 'Left Outer' and assumes that the proud possessor will be able to grasp the fact without difficulty. But it does proudly proclaim that it is Serial No. A911. Stores Ref 22C/787. Contract No. 3040 Size 9, Type 'D' and boasts an imprint of a regal crown surmounting the initials A.M. which everybody knew to stand for AIR MINISTRY.

I have carelessly abandoned these gloves in numerous crew rooms, canteens, messes and aircraft dispersal points but they have always been most promptly returned to me. No one ever wanted to swipe such an easily recognizable pair and everybody remembered the dolt who owned them. Happily when we began to be regularly occupied with night operations during the war I found that the difference in colour became less of an embarrassment, when viewed by the feeble light in and around our aircraft every kind of glove appeared to be of a dull grey colour. And now, as I picked them up in readiness for my snow clearance task, I found myself wondering exactly what sort of comment a genuine pair of war worn gloves would make if they could only speak.

I could imagine 'Left Outer' saying 'You remember how you used to stagger out to the kite at a Lincolnshire airfield on those cold dark winter nights? . . . just before midnight . . . or maybe at 2.00 AM. . . . frequently in the snow. You had your parachute pack in your left hand and your fingers would have been damned cold but for me.' 'Right Outer' would probably reply 'Doesn't that guy ever shut up? Every time you carried a pack in your left hand, you had a heavy satchel loaded with navigation gear in the other and wasn't I your right hand man? And when you pressed the button to deliver bombs, incendiaries or sea mines or whatever . . . I was always right on the ball . . . the ball of your thumb I mean.'

The act of putting the gloves on reminded me of the last time they were handed back to me which was at RAF North Luffenham on the occasion of my retirement. I had dutifully brought all my flying kit back to the Equipment Section to be struck off my charge as per regulations. All at once, the boot was on the other foot, in a manner of speaking. The vigilant equipment assistant commented 'But these are not a pair, even the labels are different, the schedule clearly says "one pair of gloves" and the deficiency will have to be charged to you, sir.' I vainly sought to pull rank and soon the section sergeant was brought into the dispute, I noticed with a tremor that they were both massively built and recalled that they were the mainstays of the local rugby football team. My throat was getting to be a little dry before I managed to get the Senior Equipment Officer drawn into the affray and it was a relief to find that he was more human. 'I know what I can do, you have had them for nearly 20 years and you say they were not new when you got them. I'll certify them as worn out and you may keep them if you wish.' He then almost threw them at me.

By this time the gentle voice was only an inch or two from my ear. 'If you stand there much longer the snow will have melted.'

Squadron Leader G. Haworth

# Definition of an 'Erk'

The Concise Oxford Dictionary defines the word 'Erk' as slang for a '*Naval Rating; Aircraftman; disliked person. (20th c.; orig unkn)*' but as everyone who has served in the RAF knows the Air Force version is quite a unique person and almost impossible to define.

An erk can be made from the raw material of an apprentice, boy entrant, air cadet or as a last resort a civilian and any resemblance between the finished product and the airman on the recruiting posters is purely coincidental.

He may be short or tall, thin or fat, there is no medium that being the term for a size of uniform which does not fit anyone without being altered.

He likes beer, girls, cigarettes, mail from home, juke box music, NAAFI breaks, pay parades and leave.

He dislikes SWOs, SPs, guard duty—especially main gate, bull night, standing in queues, kit inspections, COs and AOCs parades.

He is an authority on national defence, foreign policy, politics and sport but does not have a clue on Regulations.

He can be found inside, underneath and on top of aircraft and a variety of MT vehicles usually covered in oil whether in denims, working blue or KD (under no circumstances should he be confused with his habitual enemy known as a 'Shiney' found in the SHQ).

Apart from the hangar he can also he found in the airmens mess, NAAFI—'a non profit making organization', Astra, Gym, guardroom, out of bounds, out of luck and in the s—t.

No one can be as generous on pay day or as tight fisted the day before it.

He can combine the rare qualities of actor and story teller which only come to light when requesting compassionate leave or when arriving back late after it.

He may be surprisingly intelligent or as thick as two short planks, depending on his mood.

It's practically impossible for him to pack all his kit into a big pack, small pack, two ammo pouches, large kit bag and small kit bag, but the amount of items he can get into the pockets of a working blue has to be seen to be believed; for example a battered 1250 ('seen some service that, mate'), a chit for early dinner and late supper, a crumpled packet of cigarettes, some unanswered letters plus a dear john, a pack of cards (for losing his pay), a piece of 4 × 2, a set of irons (KF&S), and a treasured 295—to mention but a few.

He may vary in colour from white to pink, red or brown depending on the posting.

Our average erk, if there is such a thing, is equipped with five gears:

| | |
|---|---|
| 1st (Slow) | For use in getting out of bed in the morning and reporting to the guardroom for jankers after the inevitable 252. |
| 2nd (Idle) | For use when chiefy shouts 'On the (Hangar) doors two six'. |
| 3rd (Fast) | For getting out of camp on a Friday afternoon. |
| 4th (Overdrive) | For use in catching the last bus back to camp on a stomach full of beer. |
| 5th (Reverse) | For use when volunteers are requested for Duty Crash Crew. |

His vision is quite remarkable, he will trip over a sign which says 'Keep Off The Grass' while able to see an SP hiding behind a hangar up to a mile away.

With regard to enthusiasm or, to be more precise, dedication we once again have a paradox for, to the wrong type of NCO or Zobbit, an erk can be one of the most moaning, skiving, elusive individuals under the sun, while for the right kind of supervisor he will willingly work long hours in miserable weather conditions purely for the satisfaction of doing a good job and watching 'his' aircraft lift off the end of the runway.

The life-span of an erk depends on his length of training, which is rarely longer than six months and, as far as he is concerned, it ends when he sews that very apt symbol of power—the propeller—on his arm; this brings us to another unusual factor, which is, how has a solely male species with such a short life span managed to exist for over sixty years on some of the most appalling airfields in the snow, desert and jungle on (occasionally) even more appalling rations, and still survive? Possibly his sense of humour? So, despite his virtues and vices, the erk plays a unique part in the RAF which looks like continuing as long as there's an air force.

I have attempted to give a brief account of the many facets of an 'Erk', and if you are curious enough to wonder how I arrived at this definition—self analysis! How else?

Ray Crompton

# The Canberras Have Come

*By Our Special Reporter*

At Lungi Airport, February 17, 1956

Soon after, the occupants of the bombers came out and the ground crews set to work servicing the bombers. The scientific, mechanical and smart way of supplying paraffin oil was admirable. Among the attendants at Bomber WH983 was James Kent.

Vice-Air Marshal J. R. Whitley, C.B., C.B.E., D.S.O., D.F.C.

This gentleman who was in khaki was seen to be a tall man, not with any bulk of flesh.

He was simple but 'full of air' as could be seen when in conversation. Mr Whitley enjoyed the trip from Kano to Lungi which took them about 3½ hours a distance approximately of 1,500 miles. It was bumpy at one time of the voyage.

The Queen, in Nigeria, visited the Squadron and saw also a demonstration flight which was much appreciated. The trip to Nigeria and their stay there was much enjoyed: the climate was at its best.

At a height of 50,000 feet Vice-Air Marshal Whitley climbed in order to meet the situation aerial.

There was no fuss—truly great personalities make no fuss, weighted with positions, freighted with honours they go down in humility—with him and he spoke as one having that authority of common sense not common among many.

For nearly 31 years now he has been in the air and he likes the sensations. His wife and four children (boys) of whom the eldest is 22 and the youngest is 11 are at home and their minds travel now and again airwards with their husband and father respectively.

These Bombers belong to No. 9 Squadron. The trip to here was uneventful.

The members of the public could see the Canberras in flight and enjoy the sight but it is another thing to see them on the ground with all their grandeur. Each Bomber—just to give a skeleton description—has what is called Perspex forming the nose. It is transparent resembling glass. The same stuff is at the top in a sort of oval canopy or hood from which the navigator can see above. At the span of the wings are a complicated mass of mechanism from which the propulsion is effected. One saw inside the seats of the pilot and navigator with ramifications of wires, arrangements of appliances and controls regulating, somewhat, for the release of bombs by the navigator. The occupants of a Bomber are sometimes three but mostly two. Each Bomber had the figure of a bat with expanded wings looking out at each side of the helm has this with the mark IX above it in red. This shows the squadron to which they belong.

When the Bomber arrives on the ground moving on to its halting place, it does so with a whistling sound as of a Whistling tea-kettle.

Squadron Leader L. G. Bastard, in WH977 (and whose atmospheric contacts made the condensation trails) was found interesting. He flew at a height of 48,000 feet. Other interesting personalities at the airport included Flt/Lieut. Graham who was said to be in command of the Hastings that preceded the Canberras. The Press Officer Mr Gunnil was full of interest.

The Bombers were WH983 (which the Vice-Air Marshal brought) and as mentioned earlier was the first to land, WH947, WH973, WH969 and WH977.

After lapse of some time, the airmen (contingent) with their baggage travelled to Freetown.

May the beauty and skill seen in constructing and powering of these jet propelled Bombers never fail to bring the importance of British supremacy in the air, also a walking side by side with the abhorrence for war and bring before the minds eye always what the 'trap door' in each Bomber means. Sierra Leone cannot forget the historic visit of the jet propelled Bombers.

*The Daily Guardian*, Sierra Leone,
20 February 1956

# Typhoon Tribute, RAF High Ercall, July 1942

No 257 (Burma) Squadron was one of the Battle of Britain squadrons who had covered themselves in glory with Hurricanes. It even had, at one time, the famous Stanford-Tuck as CO. Its motto 'THAY MYAY GYEE SHIN SHWEE HTI', translated means 'DEATH OR GLORY'. From Honiley, the squadron was posted to High Ercall to be converted to Typhoons. The affection for the Hurricanes was such that, were it not for the fact that one of the first American fighter squadrons to come to Britain came to use the same station, mutiny would have broken out. However, to impress the Americans and to show the stiff upper lip the mutiny was converted to a 'Wake' in Wellington and everyone mislaid their station-issued bicycles in the process. Honour being served, the job of becoming familiar with Typhoons, which, to us ground crew, were ungainly, ferocious and totally alien monsters, was a problem after the sleek female-like Hurricane.

One of the main differences was the eliminating of the familiar 'trolley-acc.' and the introduction of the 'cartridge starter'. This process was the ignition in the engine of the fuel by an explosion instead of an electric spark. Slowly, the acceptance of the Typhoon became a reality and the entirely different role of the aircraft caught on and a new pride developed. As Pete Scotchmere, one of the pilots, said of the Typhoon with a certain amount of arrogance, 'You don't fly them. You aim them!'

After three months with half of the squadron fitted out with Typhoons, a new challenge presented itself to the ground crew, the first of many but nevertheless a first. For some reason, an engine change became necessary and as this was a major operation a representative from the firm of Napier, the manufacturer of the Sabre engine, was invited to check the details. The engine was duly changed and the aircraft wheeled out of the hangar for a test run and to make sure that all other functions were unimpaired by this exercise, a pilot was on hand to taxi it down to the flights. The engineering officer was on hand to either congratulate the fitters or be congratulated by the CO, who also was present. The one outstanding member of the entourage was, of course, the representative of Napier Sabre engines in his pure white overalls with a large green sabre embroidered on the left breast pocket which contained a pen, feeler gauge and micrometer. Ranging around the aircraft were the fitters who had done the job, other tradesmen involved, but in the forefront was the flight sergeant fitter himself. He was trying to fuss around the engineering officer and oversee the aircraft at the same time but was being upstaged by the corporal in charge of the engine change team.

The moment of truth arrived. Would it start? A box of cartridges was brought out—six in a box—to fill the revolving holder in the aircraft and loaded into the firing chambers. The representative declined the offer to start the engine on the grounds that this was an everyday operation and he would prefer to make his assessment whilst the engine was running. Likewise, the engineering officer and flight sergeant refused the pleasure of starting the engine so it was left to the corporal to take the plunge.

The first try produced a small cough from the engine and smiling nods were exchanged between the various dignitaries and it seemed that the whole airfield had paused in mid-action. The Americans across in the other hangar had ceased work and were watching this ceremony with interest. The rest of the maintenance unit had come to the doors of the hangar to witness the phenomenon. The second try produced nothing, the rest of the six cartridges produced no firing of the engine. The flight sergeant was getting visibly riled and told a fitter to go and get some more cartridges. He strode over to the aircraft, jumped on the wing and could be seen to tell the corporal in no uncertain terms what he thought of him, his family and his future offsprings. The corporal got out and the flight sergeant got in whilst the cartridges were loaded and, with a look of superiority at the engineering officer, proceeded to fire the cartridges one after the other in an attempt to start the engine. He eventually admitted defeat and since the engineering officer, knowing a bad bet when he saw one, refused to try, it was left to the Napier representative to take up the challenge.

He proved himself to be no duffer. Before he got into the cockpit, he had the engine cowlings removed and the engine checked and in doing so his white overall suffered. It became obvious too that the corporal and flight sergeant who had joined him were receiving from him a reprimand. He, too, failed to start the engine.

The dignitaries were getting impatient and began looking for some reason to leave but whilst the CO remained, they had to stay and like it. It had nearly reached the farcical stage with first one and then another person getting into the cockpit, firing a cartridge, getting out and making way for somebody else to take his place, without any success.

This could have gone on all day and it seemed that the CO had had enough, when, from the flights on the other side of the airfield, came a man who was well known on the squadron. His name was Cartwright. He was a fitter, not a very good one according to the very same flight sergeant who was now standing amidst the empty cartridge boxes. He had been heard to say that Cartwright couldn't put a piece of locking wire through a ring spanner. He was still an AC2, and had been for years. His appearance did nothing for him, his cap was flat on his head and was a darker blue than his tunic due to the oil it had soaked up over the years. He was chubby, quiet, but a good drinker, always a good way to judge character it was said. He paused beside the litter of cartridges spread around the Typhoon.

'Having trouble starting it, Chiefy?' he said, addressing the flight sergeant and ignoring the CO and the other officers present.

The flight sergeant muttered something not very polite to him and made a gesture out of sight of the others to indicate he should go away. This was all lost to Cartwright, who plunged in again without a tremor.

'Shall I start it for you, Chiefy?' he said, without changing his stride towards the cockpit.

The flight sergeant, who was now at the end of his tether, turned to the Napier representative, the engineering officer and the CO for some outward show of guidance. Receiving none except an amused shrug from the CO, he took this as a sign to go ahead and curtly nodded to Cartwright, who slid into the cockpit with the flight sergeant on one wing beside him and the Napier representative on the other side.

Cartwright began the preliminaries to starting the engine and in the lull that still prevailed could be heard first one remark and then another.

'That's too much "ky-gas" for . . .'

'Not so much throttle, you'll . . . .'

'Cartwright, get out of that b— cockpit or I'll . . .'

There was a cough, followed by a rumble, followed by a growl and then a full-throated roar. The flight sergeant and the Napier representative were lost in a cloud of blue smoke until cleared by the slipstream.

After this it became an anticlimax. Everyone congratulated everyone else. The engineering officer chatted to the CO as they walked away, the flight sergeant slipped off the wing, coughing, and began to have a heated argument with the Napier representative whilst the corporal replaced the cowlings and helped the pilot into the cockpit to take the Typhoon down to the flights.

Cartwright? Well, he went on to the stores, where he was going to in the first place, to get some locking wire and the war went on, with No 257 Squadron eventually receiving its full complement of Typhoons. Except that Cartwright was known after that day as 'One Cartridge Cartwright', which, in the eyes of the fitters and, as he admitted himself, was as good as a medal.

Corporal J. W. Dickenson

# The Reader's Digest

The following anecdotes are reprinted from *The Reader's Digest*

The Commanding Officer of an RAF Station was Group Captain Frost and the local Army commander a Brigadier Frost. When asked whether this caused any confusion, the Group Captain replied: 'Not really. I'm called Air Frost and he is known as Ground Frost.'

Our RAF station was in the process of changing over aircraft from Phantoms to Jaguars, whose aircrews did nothing but boast of the prowess of their 'Big Cats'. The Phantom crews took it all in good heart—but retaliation was at hand. One morning the Jaguar men came out on the tarmac to find, at the nose of each of their aircraft, a saucer of milk and, at the tail, a sand-tray.

A certain aircrew flight sergeant said to his wife, 'Don't bother about supper, I'll bring some fish and chips back as I'm only on a training flight tonight.'

During the flight, the Cyprus crisis occurred and the aircraft was diverted. Six days later, our hero arrived home. 'Where's the fish and chips?' asked his wife. 'There was a long queue,' he replied.

At an RAF camp renowned for its tough discipline my job before the annual inspection was to paint the kerbstones white. But to my horror, I accidentally knocked over the paint pot, spilling in the road a large white puddle which I couldn't obliterate. In desperation, I painted the puddle into a neat square—and thankfully my sergeant made no comment. Four years later I returned to the same camp. Not only was my square still there; it had been freshly repainted for the annual inspection.

At Aden's Khormaksar airport some years ago, a USAF major surveyed the towering Beverley transport planes lined up on the tarmac, then turned to the RAF flight lieutenant standing beside him: 'Are these the biggest aircraft you have out here?' he asked in superior tones.

'Yes, sir,' replied the flight lieutenant. 'But you should have seen the ones we brought them out in.'

Like many others in the early days of the war, the fighter pilot had lost his way and had landed unexpectedly at a remote bomber station in Lincolnshire.

Inevitably he was greeted by some good-natured teasing about his lack of navigational skill. He stoutly maintained that he had known perfectly well he was landing at a bomber station, since he could see from many miles away that everyone was wearing a Distinguished Flying Cross. Then, remembering that he would miss his usual night out in London, he remarked patronizingly. 'I don't suppose you chaps ever get up to town.' A poker-faced bomber pilot had the last word: 'Only for the investitures.'

Our RAF signal squadron stationed in Nairobi, Kenya, was delighted at the news that twelve long-awaited Land-Rovers were at last coming up the 320-mile dust road from Mombasa. One of the vehicles, however, arrived with its lamps broken, radiator grille bent, and front wings distorted.

In the inquiry which followed, the driver was brought before his squadron commander and asked to explain. 'There's nothing to say, sir, really,' he said, 'except that I hit a three-dimensional zebra crossing.'

At the dress rehearsal for the recruits' parade, several WRAF officers took the place of dignitaries who would be in attendance on the day. To indicate whom she was representing, each stand-in held a board, one of which was marked—DWRAF—Director of the Women's Royal Air Force.

'Sergeant, there's just one thing I didn't understand,' a puzzled recruit asked afterwards, 'Why was that officer pretending to be a dwarf?'

During a security check at our RAF camp one evening, the duty clerk discovered an unmarked package on the security officer's desk. Remembering warnings about suspicious objects, he called the orderly sergeant who in turn alerted the police, fire brigade and ambulance.

Standing by, they watched a policeman inspect the package, then cautiously open it—to reveal 200 leaflets on what to do if you find a suspicious object.

Some months after joining the RAF, my son decided to grow a moustache.

He was proud of its progress, until on parade one day his sergeant commented: 'What's this, laddie? One of your eyebrows come down for a drink?'

# *Tee Emm* and *RAF Journal*

## *You are Old, Air Chief Marshal*

'You are old, Air Chief Marshal,' the young P/O said,
'And your body's exceedingly fat,
Yet you fly thro' the air with the greatest of ease.
Pray what is the reason for that?'

'The cause of this strange aeronautical grace,'
Said the Boffin, relating his powers,
'Was the arduous practice in cockpit routine
And learning instructions for hours.'

'I know,' said the P/O, 'but answer me this.
I've seen you do circuits and bumps,
Yet you never come down with the undercart up,
Like me and the other poor chumps.'

'You see,' said the Marshal, with almost a smirk,
'It's habit, good training, and sense
To look round the cockpit at needles and tits,
Relax yourself; never sit tense.

'Watch the pitch and the flaps and the mixture as well,
The airspeed and angle of glide.
It's so very much simpler to land on the wheels
Than prang on the belly or side.

'Watch the chap in the band box,' the old boy next said,
'With his lights, and his lamps and his flags.
Pay regard to his gestures, his foibles and whims;
Come in gently—no zigs and no zags.

'In my youth,' said the Marshal, 'I studied each word
That Flying Control put before me—
And avoided, thereby, those ridiculous prangs,
As frankly the stupid things bore me.

'Before taking off, get your maps—sign the book;
The Form 700 as well.
Check the wind and the weather, the runway in use;
Safety first—for you never can tell.

'I taxi quite slowly with caution and care,
And watch other aircraft about;
It's foolish to argue with bowsers or trucks,
They have the last word, without doubt.

'I look after my helmet, my dinghy and 'chute—
It's true they belong to the King,
But friends who are corpses have proved more than once
To maltreat them's the craziest thing.

'I never take chances when close to the ground;
And when clouds and high hills are about,
I use my R/T for all that it's worth
And keep all my fingers well out.

'Emulate me—young man—if determined you'd be
To grow old and get covered with rings,
Always bearing in mind, 'tis your chest—not your back
Should be used for displaying your wings.'

By now our young P/O had had quite enough
And he started to yawn and to fidget. . . .
But he made up his mind that in future he'd try
To extract the proverbial digit.

*Tee Emm*, 1944

## PER ARDUA AD FORMULA
## OR
## PER FORMULA AD ASTRA . . . ?

('*The exact official translation of the RAF motto is still under discussion.*')

'PER ARDUA AD ASTRA.'
For long these words have been
The motto of our airmen,
Who don't know what they mean.

The Marshals in the Ministry,
The pilots and the crew,
They never learned much Latin
And so they can't construe.

They're modern in the Air Force,
They need no classics there,
—Even 'DE BELLO GALLICO'
Is useless in the air . . .

So withdraw their Latin motto
And they can then make shift
With '$L = C_L \frac{1}{2} \rho v^2 S$'—
The formula for . . . Lift!

*Tee Emm*, 1941

# Variations on a Theme

**A**

The door of the dispersal hut opened and three pilots with parachutes over their shoulders came in blinking at the strong light. The Intelligence Office looked up from his game of shove ha'penny.

'Any luck?'

'Not much,' replied the flight commander. He peeled off his Mae West and lit a cigarette before giving his report.

Turning to his sergeant, who by now was lost in the mysteries of *No Orchids for Miss Blandish*, the Intelligence Officer asked, 'What about you, Grimes?'

'Well, Sir, I was Tail-end Charlie and when I went in there was a hell of a lot of tracer flying about, all sorts of colours. I think it must have been Hitler's birthday or something. Then a searchlight came smelling round but I fixed him.'

'Did it dowse?'

'I'll say it did! I had another squirt at some kites dispersed near a wood and one of them started to burn. After that I pushed off home because the atmosphere wasn't too healthy.'

'Did you see any shipping?'

'Oh yes. A flakship had a crack at me but it was pretty ropey shooting so I put the rest of my ammo. into him. It was so dark I couldn't see a ruddy thing.'

The IO got some more facts out of the third pilot and sat down to send off a signal.

**B**

To H.Q.F.C. 12.12.41. Int. 7.

DUSK OFFENSIVE OPERATION REPORT. THREE SPITFIRES, Mk.Vc. No. 9999 Sqdn. TOOK OFF TANGMERE 1805 HOURS, –/12/41, LANDED 1927 HOURS. F/LT. DERWENT (CANADA) LED SECTION ON COURSE 124 DEGREES MAKING LANDFALL FIVE MILES EAST OF CALAIS AND LOCATED AERODROME AT VILLEMORT. F/LT. DERWENT ATTACKED TWO S/Ls. WHICH DOUSED ALSO LIGHT FLAK POSITION IN SAND DUNES, GRID REF. N. 1784. SGT. GRIMES (SOUTH AFRICA) ATTACKED DISPERSED AIRCRAFT ON GROUND ON NORTH SIDE OF AERODROME SETTING ONE ON FIRE. HE ALSO PUT OUT A SEARCHLIGHT AND ATTACKED FLAKSHIP WHICH HAD OPENED UP WITH INACCURATE FIRE. P/O BROWN SAW STRIKES FROM HIS CANNON SHELLS ON A HANGAR AND A SMALL FIRE BROKE OUT. THERE WAS INTENSE LIGHT FLAK FROM NORTH AND WEST SIDE OF AERODROME MOSTLY RED OR GREEN TRACER. FULL RESULTS NOT OBSERVED OWING TO POOR VISIBILITY. OUR CASUALTIES PILOTS NIL, AIRCRAFT NIL. SECRET, IMMEDIATE.
T.O.R. 2000.

**C**

**NASTY NIGHT FOR NAZIS**

*By the Daily Reflector air correspondent*

Screaming out of inky blackness Spitfire pilots rained death and destruction on enemy airfields last night. The attack, carried out by a strong force, was led by ace Canadian pilot F/Lt 'Johnny' Derwent, who is engaged to vivacious Miss Violet Nash, famous Bermondsey beauty queen. 'I think Jack is wonderful,' said Miss Nash when interviewed at her West End flat today.

Diving at breathless speed through a terrific barrage of many hued tracer shells and 'flaming onions' our fighters skimmed the tree tops, the wind screaming though their struts and bracing wires. A hail of withering fire belched from their formidable array of cannon and machine guns, destroying enemy planes cunningly concealed in the trees, knocking out AA guns and shattering searchlight concentrations. Hangars were left in ruins and fires started which could be seen by watchers on the cliffs at Dover. 'Johnny' Derwent said you could have read a newspaper by them. All our.aircraft returned safely from these and other operations.

**D**

Extract from *The Times*

A Berlin communiqué reads as follows:—Last night the enemy despatched ineffective patrols over occupied territory. No damage or casualties were caused. Seven British aircraft were destroyed by our defences without loss to ourselves.

*RAF Journal*, 1942

# *The Awful Tale of PO Prune*

This is the tale of PO Prune,
Now in hospital at Frome,
Who, though Industrious and Keen,
The type who keeps his buttons clean,
Earned for himself a bitter fate,
Because he could not concentrate.
Although he always tried his best
To be Efficient (like the rest),
He simply hadn't got the skill
To concentrate on COCKPIT DRILL.

He tried mnemonics; used to sit
For ages memorising it.
But once inside his aeroplane,
He just forgot it all again.

The inter-com, the airscrew pitch,
The warning indicator switch,
The flaps, and elevator trim,
Were one and all alike to him.

He happened then in course of time
To muddle up this pantomime,
Whilst coming in to land one day
In (what he thought) the usual way.
He accidentally pulled the catch,
That jettisons the exit hatch.
It quite surprised him when he saw
His gunner vanish through the floor,
Then hurtle downwards through the air, –
To burst beside the signal square.
Poor PO Prune in pensive mood,
Forgot to check his altitood,
And at a hundred miles per hour
He cannoned off the water tower,
Mowed down an Orderly Parade,
Then hit the deck and ricochetted
Right through the Mess, wherein a bunch
Of Officers were taking lunch.
Imagine then the screams and groans,
The crunching sound of splintered bones,
The shattered glass, the ruptured seams,
The tangled mass of twisted beams,
The *débris* scattered everywhere.
It was a Terrible affair.
When all was clear they took the dead
And heaped them in the tractor shed,
They counted them and found at length
That fully half the ration strength
Were incapacitated, or
Revolting messes on the floor.
From 'midst the havoc he had wrought
They dug Prune from his Juggernaut.
The doctor hastily arrived—
And found, alas, he had *survived.*
Next day Group Captain Cholmondly-Pym
Severely reprimanded him;
A punishment both wise and just,
For pilots in the Service must
(Lest they should share PO Prune's fate)
Be capable
and CONCENTRATE.

*Tee Emm*, 1942

# Basic English in West Africa

The following letter was received by the Transport Manager, Elder-Dempster Lines, Lagos, after the fall of a native from the top of a 'C' class flying-boat into a lighter during loading operations.

Sir,—My statement to you about my speech to my lawyer when he came to demand as per legal order the sum of £50 for my poor damaged body falling in company's lighter while doing my honest duty, on account of which I might have gone to heaven that day.

Praise the Lord I did not go. But Sir, when you said to my legal adviser first, that I was drunk, second that the cause was stealing gin from lighter, well Sir, these two speeches prove that you are the son of the father of lies, that is the Devil, because –

1. Said gin had been freely drunk at 8 a.m. prompt.
2. I fell heavily in the lighter at 11 a.m. prompt.
3. At 11 a.m. gin had been passed through body so cause of top heaviness has finished.

Therefore you are the very first born of the Father of lies, that is Devil because second charge of stealing company's gin is libel, because Sir, do not take away my poor character, because £1,000 is often lost legal by libel. As legal costs plenty of money Sir, for God's sake try and sign for £50 for damage to my poor frame of mortality as follows:–

Fell head down on lighter on tons of metal.
One head splitten.
One nose useless (very grave).
One shoulder broken (blood extracted).
One arm bent (blood extracted).
One thick leg dashed.
One half leg broken (bloody freely).

Now Sir, these hurts are cheap at £50. Please Sir, for God's sake sign when I will pay you £15, not as a bribe Sir, No, I do not sin like that, but to show you thanks and the Lord for complete recovery.

I will come for book re £50 in the morning, meanwhile may God watch and protect over your slumbers tonight, so as to keep you safe till morning and I get £50. May his mercy keep and protect you from the Father of lies, said Devil.

'Your Servant.'
*RAF Journal*, 1942

# *Family Pride—New Style*

At last (I can hardly believe it is true)
My daughter's a full ACW 2.
She has sampled already some WAAF institutions—
(At Gl--c–ster the chief one, it seems, is 'ablushions.')
She's been given two tunics—(and one of them fits),
Not to mention two skirts which just hold when she sits.
Her buttons put Phoebus, his glories, to shame
And shed lustre untold on the family name.
Her salute, I should judge from advance indications,
Will shake the Air Force to its very foundations.
At M–rec–mbe they showed her how fast one can march
When fully expanded by masses of starch.

And now the *pièce de resistance* is staged,
For she's crowned her achievements by getting engaged.

ENVOI

We're not, as a family, given to side,
But we feel that we *have* got some reason for pride.
Your son's a Group Captain?—Well, tumty to you!
My daughter's a full ACW 2!

*RAF Journal*, 1942

## 'Airmen, Laughing, 3,000 of'

I was a 'Kriegie' for four years. What is a Kriegie? you may ask. Well, it is short for *Kriegsgefangene*, German for prisoner-of-war. Looking back, I can find so many things that amuse me that the unpleasant side of the business seems to have died a natural death. I should have been the last to admit this, at the time when we were being caught up by Monty's armies in the far north of Germany, but that's over now.

The first few months of captivity were the most difficult. The standard of living was far below anything we had imagined, but it was not unbearable. We learned to adjust ourselves to the conditions, and we soon realized that the life would be largely what we made it. It was a great help to us that the average German was completely lacking in humour. A German can actually be embarrassed by hearty laughter. We Kriegies discovered this in the early years, and it was one of our strongest weapons to the end. For instance, it was customary for the Germans to announce punishments on the morning parades, and at each announcement 3,000 men would burst into prolonged cheers and hearty laughter. Men under guard, on their way to solitary confinement, would receive a round of applause. They would respond with a wave of the hand. A cut in the food rations would be greeted with rapturous applause. From our point of view the punishments were *not* funny, but the German reaction to our laughter certainly was. I remember a Major Jacob, a glassy-eyed, stiff-necked little man, ordering the British camp leader to announce that our 'invasion' had failed at Dieppe with heavy losses. We could not know that this was not a terrible defeat, but he looked such a self-satisfied little German. There was a moment's silence and then we let him have it—a thunderous roar of cheering. It might have been VE-Day, and Jacob looked around in bewilderment. The parade-ground was a seething mass of apparently delighted prisoners. He shuffled uncomfortably, made a few Donald Duck gestures in protest, and then looked quite dejected about the whole thing. We did not know what had happened at Dieppe, but we thought the demonstration was well worth the effort.

Warrant Officer A. J. Dixon,
*RAF Journal*, 1945

# *I Vish . . .*

*TEE EMM is proud to announce the appearance in its pages for the first time of a contribution from Germany. It is by Ober-Leutnant Otto Schitzenheimer of the German Air Force.*

With large steins of lager beer (Ersatz) in view,
Two Jerries sat talking—the subject was *YOU*.
One said, 'Fritz, you know I'm a night-fighter guy,
And nightly to strafe British bombers I try,
But I *vish* they'd fly level and straight as can be—
It makes things so very much simpler for me.
I *vish*, when I shoot at them, quarter or beam,
They vouldn't turn in, dodging my bullet stream.
I *vish* they'd all turn away *from* my attack—
There'd be more British bombers who vouldn't get back.
I *vish*, when their gunners are veary of eye,
They vouldn't still search every inch of the sky.
I *vish* they'd *all* bomb from incredible heights,
I shouldn't have nearly so many blank nights.
I *vish* they'd not *all* fly along the same route—
I've a veakness for stragglers, they're easy to shoot.
Ven the moon on the clouds makes the background all vite,
I *vish* they'd hug cloud-top, that suits me just right.
I *vish* they'd ignore what the 'old hands' all say—
They'd be easier targets—I *like* it that vay.'

*Tee Emm*, 1942

# *After Wordsworth*

I wandered lonely as a cloud,
That floats on high in straggling bits,
    When all at once I saw a crowd—
    A host of yellow Messerschmits.
    And now, interned for the duration,
    I wish I had not lost formation.

*Tee Emm*, 1942

# Poems and Songs

## *Ode to the Fallen*

Now Bert, he was a civvy,
Quite contented with his lot;
And regularly each evening
To the 'local' he would trot.

He never needed champagne
To fill him with good cheer;
A pipe or two was all he asked
And tankards full of beer.

He never went out dancing,
For a steady lad was Bert;
And he never dreamed of chasing
After little bits of skirt.

But when he joined the Air Force,
Things soon began to alter.
And once he met a wizard WAAF,
Who caused his heart to falter.

He really went a bundle on
This WAAF, whose name was Peg.
*He* said it was her girlish charm
(But it was 'oomph' and leg).

He used to go and meet her,
His hair all sleek and greased.
Boots all brushed, and buttons bright
His trousers nicely creased.

But alas for our poor hero,
One night into the bar
There stepped a man whose shoulder bore
Just one word—'CANADA'.

Poor Bert was quite dumbfounded,
And sat there partly dazed.
He couldn't get a look-in as
At Canuck Peggy gazed.

Suspense was nearing fever-heat,
The clock got near to ten.
Old Bert was fighting gamely,
'Twas neck and neck, and then—

Mother Nature called him,
But Bert he heeded not.
Until at last, to his dismay,
He had to up and trot.

As soon as he was through the door
His rival seized his chance;
He moved right in on Peggy
And 'bang' went Bert's romance.

So, for others' future guidance
The moral is quite clear:
If you want to go out flirting
Then you'll have to skip the beer.

Bas Cowlishaw, 1943

## *Hoots!*

I felt a 'coot'
In a civvy suit;
It did not suit
My style, to boot.

When boys did hoot
And throw old fruit,
The point was moot
That I did scoot
And change my suit
And my pursuit.

So now I shoot
Thro' skies all soot
With 'flak'. I hoot
And stamp my foot
And holler, 'Shoot',
When Jerries scoot
Across Flight-Lieut.
And singe his boot!

My gun goes 'Toot!'—
Jerry's 'No goot!'

One can't refute
My change of suit
Makes me feel cute!

BANG! Crash! 'Galoot!'
My 'plane's 'caput.'
Gosh!
where
the
hell's
my
p
a
r
a
c
h
u
t
e
?

## *The Unkindest Defence Cut of All* circa *1975*

I'm the last man left in the Air Force
I've an office in MoD
And a copy of Queen's Regulations
Which only apply to me
I can post myself to Leuchars
And detach me from there to Kinloss
Or send me on courses to MOTU
Then cancel the lot—I'm the boss.

I'm the last man left in the Air Force,
But the great parliamentary brains
Omitted, when cancelling people
To sell off the Stations and Planes.
The result is my inventory bulges
With KD and camp-stools and Quarters
Plus a signed book of verses by Trenchard
Which I keep for impressing reporters.

I'm the last man left in the Air Force,
I suppose you imagine it's great
To be master of all you survey, but
I tell you it's difficult, mate

I inspected three units last Thursday
As C-in-C (Acting) of Strike,
Then I swept half the runway at Laarbruch
And repaired Saxa Vord's station bike.

I'm the last man left in the Air Force,
It's not doing a lot for my health
Station Sports Days are frankly exhausting
When the Victor Ludorum's oneself.
On guest nights the Mess is so lonely,
There are times when I wish I was able
To pass the port to the chap on my left
Without seeing it fall off the table.

I'm the last man left in the Air Force,
It's quiet—but, that apart
There are plenty worse off, for example
The Only Sea Lord, for a start
He was called out last Wednesday evening
(Joint Ops with the Army, my oath)
But their rowing boat sank in the Channel
Which obliged me to rescue them both.

I'm the last man left in the Air Force
My wife says I'm never at home
When I'm not flying Hercs, I'm at Manston
Laying gallons and gallons of foam.
Or I'm in my marine craft off Plymouth
Shooting flares at the crowds on the Ho,
Or I'm Orderly Corporal at Luqa
It's an interesting life, but all go.

I'm the last man in the Air Force
I'm ADC to the Queen
I'm Duty Clerk at St Mawgan
I'm the RAF Rugby Team
Tomorrow I'm planning a guardroom
And air-testing several planes
The day after that I'm for London
To preach at St Clement Danes.

I'm the last man in the Air Force
And I'm due to go out before long
There's been no talk of any replacement
And I won't even let me sign on.
I hope to enjoy my retirement
I've put up a fairly good show
And I won't cut myself off entirely
There are always reunions, you know.

# *RAF Cadet College, Cranwell, 1924*

*Tune: 'The Lincolnshire Poacher'*

I joined the RAF as an aircrafthand as good as good could be,
But after a month my Conduct Sheet was one of the sights to see;
It was full of fines and days in Quod my Leader gave to me,
I was five times up to the Wing Commo and twice to the AOC.
So—I started again as an $A/C_2$, and now I'm an $A/C_3$.

# *A Naafi Girl*

Once there was a Naafi Girl
  And she was dressed in blue, Sir,
And in her little Institute
  She kept a bomber crew, Sir.
She kept a bomber crew, my lads,
  And kept the camp alive-o,
And when she shouted 'Contact!'
  All the bombers had to dive-o.

She said to Skipper Bill one day,
  'O come now will you fly me
Upon an operation in
  Your Wimpey o'er the high sea?'
'It's right against KR,' said he,
  'But for you I will risk it—
You'd better make your will right now—
  My Love, you take the biscuit.'

So then our little Naafi Girl
  Dressed herself in brown, Sir,
Administered a spot of rouge
  And took her face to town, Sir.
She loaded up her mobile van
  With tea and buns all ready,
And drove out to dispersal
  To the Wimpey 'F for Freddie'.

She then filled up the kite with wads
  And urns of Naafi tea, Sir,
She stored them all away in there
  As neatly as could be, Sir.
And then she put her greatcoat on
  (Careful of her kitting),
She hid herself in the fuselage
  And passed the time by knitting.

Soon Skipper Bill and all his crew
  Arrived out on dispersal.
They'd done their NFT that morn
  And needed no rehearsal.
The kite took off right merrily,
  All bombed up and quite slick-o,
And when they reached the open sea
  Our Naafi Girl was sick-o.

But she'd recovered by the time
  They reached their destined target,
Though it did not remind her of
  A pleasure trip to Margate.
The flak came up as thick as mud,
  They'd got the range for certain,
And if Bill hadn't kept his head
  That Wimpey'd gone for a Burton.

Our Naafi Girl then did her stuff,
  Inspired by the Gods, Sir,
She jettisoned the urns of tea
  And started dropping wads, Sir.
Right o'er the target they went down,
  Into the fires all burning,
And she'd released the whole darn lot
  When the kite was homeward turning.

That target looked like hell let loose,
  She'd pranged it off the map, Sir,
The flames roared up from the black below,
  She'd given it the strap, Sir.
Explosions threw the kite about,
  They'd blown up the whole place, Sir.
And when Bill saw what she had done.
  He set the course for base, Sir.

Now none else knows about this spree,
  Of that there is no doubt, Sir.
But honestly I've told you how
  That target was wiped out, Sir.
The boys all got the DFC,
  And the Naafi Girl was wed-o
To Bill the valiant skipper
  Of the Wimpey 'F for Fred-o'.

Cranwell, *circa* 1942

## *Oh! Mary, This WAAF*

*Tune: 'The Mountains of Mourne'*

Oh! Mary, this Waaf is a wonderful life,
Sure you might get a job as an officer's wife.
There are plenty of airwomen digging for gold,
At least, when I asked 'em, it's what I was told.
So I soon took a hand in this digging, y'ken,
And I tried very hard to attract all the men,
I saluted quite smartly by winking one eye,
But ignored all the airmen unless they could fly.

A young Flight Lieutenant was the cause of my fall,
So handsome, attractive and heavenly tall,
Took me for a ride in his little MG,
When something went wrong with the engine, y'see.
We were running on Pool and 100 octane,
Though I shouted quite loudly no help could obtain.
He'd twenty EAs to his credit already,
So one little Waaf couldn't make him unsteady.

And now on my story I will not enlarge,
Sufficient to say how I got my discharge.

## *Ode to the WOP/AG**

It takes guts to be a WOP/AG
And sit out in the tail
When the Focke-Wulfs are coming in
And the slugs begin to hail.

The pilot's just a chauffeur
As he only flies the plane,
We do all the . . . . . . fighting
And take all the . . . . . blame.

We have all the shooting
At these . . . . . Axis swine,
All the pilot ever shoots
Is his horrible . . . . . . line.

The pilot and observer
Each has his tons of room,
We're caged in a . . . . turret
And it's like a . . . . . . . tomb.

When the . . . . . . flak gets sticky,
And things are looking hot,
The pilot hopes his WOP/AG
Will save the . . . . . . . . . . lot.

Then if the kite should ditch itself
Into the raging sea,
Who throws the . . . . . . . . dinghy out?
The poor old WOP/AG.

And when we're on the ocean
With a hundred miles to go,
The pilot yells at his WOP/AG
'Row, you . . . . . . . . . . . . Row!'

Then when each trip is over
And the crew to the mess all fly,
You'll find the poor old WOP/AG
Still doing his DI.

But when its cleaning Browning guns,
The Observer's always late,
He does not seem to realise
That he's the Gunner's Mate.

But when this war is over,
And they add the final score,
They'll find it was the WOP/AG
Who won this . . . . . . war.

So hail then to the WOP/AG
For he's the best of man.
If he can't bring the aircraft back;
NO OTHER . . . . . . . CAN!

Dave Webster, No 38 Squadron

**Wireless Operator/Air Gunner*

# *Flight Engineer: Post War*

Now when this war is o'er and done,
Perhaps by nineteen fifty-one,
There'll come a cry from some small lad:
'Tell us a bed-time story, Dad!'

Then sadly reaching from a shelf
A book which notes not dwarf nor elf.
Dad slowly reads from faded leaves
Of Wing Tip and the Vortices.

And other gen the notes unfold
Before the tale is fully told;
The loss of lift at tip of wing,
Defeated by the Flying Ring.

When cruising for the greatest range
The IAS must never change;
Except you know when bombs are gone,
And then you choose a lower one.

Economy in mixture strength
Has often been discussed at length;
Full tanks last longest using 'Weak',
In 'Rich' you think they've sprung a leak.

Now bombers are not flown for pleasure
With Revs and Boost fixed at your leisure;
Boost must be high and Revs quite low,
If flying furthest you would go.

Endurance cruising is a bind,
Its rules stick in the simplest mind.
The first one's short; you just 'Fly Slow',
The second's shorter still; 'Fly Low.'

And now you bear in mind, my lad,
What happened to your poor old Dad:
For scoffing at these tales of flight,
He ended up a Stalag mite.

Flight Lieutenant J. Roughley,
RAF St Athan, 1944

## *Ode to an Odious Place*

In days gone by
When I was riled,
A wicked curse I'd utter –
'Oh go to Hell,' I'd bravely say,
But only in a mutter.

The years have passed,
I've travelled far
And evil thoughts I've housed,
So 'Go to Aden' now I roar,
Whenever I'm aroused.

The reason why I will explain,
If you've never served in Aden,
It's the most malodorous place on earth,
Yet they say 'twas the Garden of Eden.

So now we know the mystery
That always seemed so odd,
Why Cain slew Abel and took himself
Into the Land of Nod.

Pat Milne, a Service wife,
RAF Steamer Point, 1963

## 'Our Norm'

This is the tale of Norman Slade,
Young and handsome, British-made,
Who served his country well and true,
Back in nineteen-forty-two.

Phones rang up and down Whitehall,
When Norman answered the nation's call,
And Churchill said, 'Gad, that dream was bad,
A voice saying "Get thee over lad".'

The Army closed its serried ranks,
The Navy said they'd manage thanks,
But the Air Force smiled, said, 'Heaven sent,
We're one man short in the Regiment.'

So off went Norm to join the erks,
With little or nowt in the way of perks,
But he said, 'We'll soon have changes made . . .
Like a de-mob fund for AC Slade.'

He learned to Order, Present and Slope,
Swung about on the end of a rope,
But the last straw came when they shoved him over
A cliff as high as the ones at Dover.

He hovered over Whitley Bay,
Like the Fairy Queen in a Christmas play,
Hanging bits of wire about,
That were supposed to keep the Germans out.

He got fed up with ten-mile marches,
Heavy boots and aching arches,
Said, 'It's wheels I want to put my feet on.'
Next thing he knew . . . he was outside Weeton!

On the next few weeks, best draw a veil,
On gloom of such gigantic scale,
But for miles around sounding loud and clear,
Came a voice that called 'Get me out of 'ere.'

Then one fine day the gates clanged wider,
And Slade emerged . . . a Despatch Rider.
At last he'd come into his own,
With the whole of England in which to roam.

He beat up Hendon and Watford Way,
Cambridge chose Romans any day,
He woke Down Ampney and destroyed its calm,
And shook 'em rigid round Blakehill Farm.

He toted a gun with one up the spout,
Sold civvies back fruit that had cost him nowt,
And when sergeants shouted 'On parade',
They all fell in . . . except for Slade.

He supervised the cookhouse ranges,
Gained control of the 'phone exchanges,
And if the CO felt in doubt,
He'd say, 'Ask Slade what it's all about.'

But once he'd dealt with his own affairs,
He'd often help the RAF with theirs,
Bringing about the total collapse,
Of first the Jerries, and then the Japs.

When word went round among the mob,
That the day had dawned for Norm's demob,
Group Captains sighed, said, 'It's all right Jack,
Slade has given the Air Force back.'

## *This Afternoon We Burned Our Files*

With nods and becks and wreathed smiles,
this afternoon we burned out files.
They told us we could only keep,
what could be carried in a jeep,
but when we've got our bed rolls in,
and packed the old chye swindle tin,
the space that's left is far too small,
to carry any files at all,
and so we took each file we'd got,
and sacrificed the ruddy lot.

It is not often that a clerk,
can leave his desk for such a lark,
but I for one would never tire,
of casting files upon a fire.
To stop the papers blowing round,
we dug a deep hole in the ground,

and to be sure that they would catch,
poured petrol on and struck a match.
What Joy, what unimagined bliss,
to hear the whole combustion hiss.
What other climax, what elation,
can compare with this cremation?
The greatest moment of our lives,
the arson of admin's archives.

See the stiff red covers wrinkle,
watch the papers catch and crinkle.
Now they've vanished with the flames,
and all their silly pompous names,
Receipt and issues, Stocks at parks,
Orders for the Duty Clerks,
Battle Orders and locations,
Establishments at Delta station.
Aircraft—Blenheims and Marauders,
Middle East Accounting orders.
And last of all the fat extraneous,
Correspondence Miscellaneous.
All gone and now we've got a box,
To keep our underclothes and socks.

The filing system's in the grave,
and we no more can be its slave.
Nor will there ever be a stir,
if signals come which cross-refer.
If we don't know what they're about,
we'll never book the blighters out.

And now, we thought, we all stand equal,
but the story has a sequel,
for of course there came one day,
a signal for the AOA,
and written right beside the date,
was Ref. my T.Q 68.

The harrassed duty clerk said *?&? it,
I've no files and I can't flag it,
and unsuspecting took it in,
the AOA turned black as sin and said
in mortifying style: 'I want to see the ruddy file.'

From here of course the story's plain.
We've opened all our files again,
and no longer have we got a box,
to keep our underclothes and socks.

# *Albert and the Corporal*

There's an airport somewhere near Geneifa,
With its share of red tape and bull,
Where aircraftsman Albert Ramsbottom,
Arrived with his kitbag chock full.

A fine little chap was young Albert,
Dressed up in best blue, quite a swell,
With his cane with its crest-mounted handle,
The finest the NAAFI could sell.

Though he didn't think much of his quarters,
His bed space was draughty and small,
No easy chairs by the fireside,
'Cause there was no fireside at all.

So seeking for amusement
He found the canteen o'er the way,
Where blokes muck about on piano,
And keep all the custom away.

He found there a Corporal called Crasher,
On his arm was a chevron two bar,
He stood in an elegant posture
With his elbows a-resting on bar.

Now Albert had heard talk about Corporals,
And as how they were terrifically bad;
To see Crasher looking so peaceful like,
It didn't seem right to the lad.

So straight away the brave little fellow,
Not showing a morsel of fear,
Took his cane with its crest-mounted handle
And pushed it right in Corporal's ear.

You could see that Corporal didn't like it,
For giving a kind of a roar,
Run him right down to the guardroom
And put him in cell and locked door.

His pals who had seen the occurrence
Didn't know what to do next,
Till someone said, 'Sarge, Crasher's mushed out young Albert.'
Sergeant said, 'Hee, I am vexed.'

Flight Commander had to be sent for,
He said, 'What's all this to do?'
Sergeant told what had happened to Corporal,
And proved it by ear black and blue.

Flight Commander he wanted no bother.
He hardly knew just what to say,
And suggested, 'Let's settle this matter,
With some extra fatigues for the day.'

At this Corporal got a bit awkward
And said, 'No, no, that won't do.
Someone has got to charge him,'
So he pulled out a Form 252.

The CO then gave his opinion
That no one was really to blame,
And hoped Corporal's ear would get better
And once more be normal again.

At this Corporal got proper blazing.
'Thank you, sir, kindly,' said he,
'What! Spend all me time being target
For blinking young airmen? Not me!'

(With apologies to Stanley Holloway)

# *Ye Book of Rules For Flying Fools*

**1.** As is the telephone operator who giveth the wrong number, so is he who extolleth his exploits in the air.

**2.** For I have watched him do his stuff on the ground; Lo, for an hour have I heard him talk of himself, till he thinkest he is the best pilot ever.

**3.** He is like unto a woman who knowest not how to say good-bye on the telephone; and the truth is not in him.

**4.** Though he be as honest as a child in all else, yet will he lie about his aerial adventures. His chest protrudeth and he maketh other men to be weary.

**5.** He shall enlarge upon the dangers of his adventures, but in my sleeve shall be heard the tinkling of silvery laughter.

**6.** Verily, men do foolish things thoughtlessly, knowing not why, but an aeroplane doeth naught without reason.

**7.** Let not thy familiarity with aeroplanes breed contempt, lest thou become exceedingly careless at a time when great care is necessary to thy well-being.

**8.** A wise pilot scenteth trouble afar and avoideth a forced landing in the waste spaces.

**9.** My son, obey the law and observe prudence, spin thou not lower than 1,500 cubits nor stunt above thine own domicile. For the hand of the law is heavy and reacheth far and wide throughout the land.

**10.** Incur not the wrath of those in authority by breaking their rules; for he who maketh right-hand circuits shall be cast out into outer darkness and whoso flyeth over football games shall be forever damned.

**11.** Let not thy prowess in the air persuade thee that others cannot do even as thou doest; for he that showeth off in public places is an abomination unto his fellow pilots.

**12.** More praiseworthy is he who can touch tail, skid and wheels to earth at one time, than he who loopeth and rolleth till some damsel stand in amaze at his daring.

**13.** He who breaketh an undercarriage in a forced landing may in time be forgiven, but he who taxieth into another's plane shall be despised for ever.

**14.** Beware the man who taketh off without looking behind him, for there is no health in him; verily I say unto you, his days are numbered.

**15.** My son, another student pilot shall come unto thee, saying, hearken not unto the words of thy great grandfather, for he doteth; list to me while I tell thee how thou shouldst do so and so.

**16.** But a little knowledge is oft-times of great danger, and thou knowest full well that my teachings are founded on much experience.

**17.** Clever men taketh the reproofs of their instructor in the same wise, one like unto another; with witty jest, confessing their dumbness and regarding themselves with humour. Yet they try again, profiting by his wise counsel and taking not offence at aught that is said.

**18.** For who so harkeneth to his precepts shall fly in safety, and shall be quiet from fear of trouble.

**19.** A reproof entereth more into a pilot of sense than an hundred compliments into a fool.

**20.** Mark a lady pilot, how she acquireth a fondness for pants; yea, though she be otherwise modest, yet doth she dress herself in ungodly raiment, displaying her limbs. Though she clotheth herself in breeches, yet doth she wear high-heeled shoes always. Her mirror must know her naught, else would she refrain from masculine attire.

**21.** Though she fly alone at great heights, yet is her powder puff close to her hand; her appearance causeth her more concern than the running of her engine.

**22.** Knoweth thou a pilot who criticizeth not another pilot's flying? I say unto you, there is not one who cannot point out another's faults and advise him, what he should do.

**23.** Better is a dancing partner with two left feet than he who laggeth behind in a formation and keepeth not his appointed place; for the leader breedeth wild thoughts.

**24.** As a wet dog who shaketh himself beside thee, so also is a pilot who usurpeth thy rightful place when landing from a formation. Woe be unto him who landeth before the leader.

**25.** Though the leader taketh thee over a city at low altitudes having no regard for thy personal safety, yet wilt thou follow him closely; but on the ground wilt thou revile him after.

**26.** As a plate of cold soup, yea, even as a kiss from one's sister, so also is a flight without a purpose or objectives; it lacketh a kick.

**27.** As a postage stamp which lacketh its glue, so are words of caution to a fool; they stick not, going in one ear and out of the other, for there is nothing between to stop them.

**28.** If thine instructor shouldest say unto thee, take thou this 'plane for it is as good as the one of thy choice, then shall thou listen politely but ignore his counsel.

**29.** For if thou wouldst do well in competitions, see that thou hast the plane which thou thinkest thou can fly with greatest ease.

**30.** My son, hearken unto my teachings and forsake not the laws of prudence, for the reckless shall not inhabit the earth for long.

**31.** Hear instruction and be wise, and refuse it not; thus wilt thou fly safely; length of days and long life and peace shall be added to thee.

## *Mild and Bitter*

One day when swimming in the sea, and all alone am I,
I meets a lovely lady who is sweet as sugar pie.
She swims around with me awhile and sits upon the sand,
And as we're sitting chatting there, she squeezes of my 'and.

She says, 'I'll go and change now, 'cos I sometimes dress, my dear,'
So I puts on my uniform and waits around quite near,
She comes back looking very neat, then pulls up with a jerk—
'Struth,' she says, and 'Cor,' she says, 'Are you a bloomin' erk?'

'Well, yes, Miss,' I replies, quite sad, 'I am, as you can see,'
And 'Well,' she says, 'That bein' so, you ain't the type for me.
I thought you was a civvy, or a officer at least,
Who'd show me 'ow a girl can 'ave a good time in the East.

'Now if you was a civvy bloke, you'd be OK by me;
Of afternoons I'd come around for a cosy chat an' tea,
At nights we'd get about the town, and week-ends we could go
In your big car up-country, to a planter's bungalow.

'Or if you was a officer, I'd stick right by your side,
Because for half the month, at least, in taxis we could ride:
You'd take me round the night club bars, in posh hotels we'd eat,
"My wife at home won't mind a bit," you'd tell me very sweet.

'And if you was a sergeant, why, I'd be your little honey,
Because you would have other things if you was short of money;
I likes a man wot's got a lot of doodahs on 'is jacket—
I know, I know, per'aps you're right, per'aps it is a racket.

'But seein' as you're just an 'erk, well what's a girl to do?
I'll guess I'll have to skin yer for yer little chip or two!
So, seein' as you're lonely for a girl friend's company.
Just for a treat, and just this once, I'll come with you to tea.'

N.B. —
And now I'm feeling nasty! Feel I'd like to have a say,
But why should I? 'Cos well I know, there'll come another day,
When astrolling round the 'dilly or up and down the Strand,
She'll only be too glad to have an 'erk to hold her hand.

*Airflow* magazine,
Ceylon, April 1945

# *Sweet and Lovely*

I'm the girl he tried to make when sitting on the shore,
Believe it or believe it not, I didn't touch his paw.
As you may guess, my hands were full to stop the little hound
From squeezing something else when there were other people round.

Surprise at finding out his type can hardly be a sin
I'm telling you I was took back, the shock was genuine.
If he was erk or Commodore I didn't give a hoot,
But, oh my dears, the dreadful line that feller tried to shoot!

Of civvy types and other men to talk I hain't inclined,
I'll just say this to girls like me they're always very kind.
But we ain't quite entirely dumb, you silly little cuss,
And those who try what you tried on are D.O.Ms. to us.

Of married men, as all girls know, it's obvious at once
That if they try their luck at all, they're up to all the stunts,
Which isn't pleasant thinkin' so we try to keep our senses,
And slap 'em down, as I did you, for rushing at their fences.

We can't help feeling sorry for the wife who's left behind,
Because it can't be pleasant to be married to that kind,
As you so generously point out, I know where it would land me:
And we've all heard that one about, 'My wife don't understand me.'

Of officers and sergeants and of erks it's quite enough
To say that with them all a girl has got to know her stuff.
There's some are good, and some are bad, and some a girl could fall for,
But most of 'em are up to tricks which I can see no call for.

They'll paw a bit, if they're that type, and try a kiss or two
And shoot a line and, in a jiff, it's 'Up them stairs with you.'
And then you know what 'appens, or at least you bloomin' ought
I see you've got a nice black eye, you nasty little sport.

N.B. —
So you see you little 'twerp' with your silly doggerel
There's girls around the place can try their hand at rhymes as well.
You nasty little horror, haven't you the sense to see
They tell the world your sort of mind, those 'cracks' in that N.B.

## *The Tale of Gertrude Glopp*

This is the tale of Gertrude Glopp,
An ACW Wireless Op,
Who feeling one day cheesed with morse
Applied for a pre-commission course.
She was duly interviewed and succeeded
Convincing them she was the type they needed.
And so she was posted to 'No 7',
The nicest station this side of heaven.

But there alas her troubles started
And six months passed ere she departed.
They crammed into the poor girl's dome
The laws of Faraday and Ohm.
They made her learn—with great reluctance—
The formula for self-inductance.
And 'DIA over DVG'
And 'One over two Pi root LC'.
They talked to her for hours on end
Of leaky grid and anode bend.
They made her draw the queerest things
Equals, and squiggly lines, and springs.
They called them 'C' and 'R' and 'L'.
But what it meant no-one could tell.
They spoke with such a knowing air
'Twas enough to make a girl despair.

But Gert was of the bulldog breed,
She found a sure way to succeed.
Each evening, prompt at half-past six,
While others went off to the flicks,
She came back to school for extra tuition,
And that's how Gertie got her commission.
In the final lists the name of Glopp,
Appeared by a handsome margin—top.

At Windermere we next find Gert,
Her head held high, her eyes alert,
Learning to bawl across the square,
To move a squad from here to there,
To administer the Air Force Act,
With justice, firmness, yet with tact,
To know when, and when not, to talk,
And to eat a rissole with a fork.

The progress of our tale has brought us
Now to a bomber base Headquarters,
Where a truly pukka signals type,
Whose name was Squadron Leader Snipe,
Was BSO of this HQ
(Base signals officer to you)
Tall and slim and dark was he—
In stockinged feet full six foot three
And a moustache clothed his upper lip
Nine inches long from tip to tip,
Curled and waxed, one might observe
In a beautiful sinusoidal curve.

One afternoon at half past four,
He heard a knock on his office door.
Next moment to his vast surprise
A lovely vision met his eyes:
In brand-new blue straight from the shop—
Assistant Section Officer Glopp.
'Reporting, Sir,' she said, 'for duty'.
But he quite dazzled by her beauty,
Leapt from his chair with a startled cry
And in confusion dropped his eye,
His visage turned quite panchromatic
And the ends of his moustache gave off static.
The truth it was that Cupid's dart,
Had smitten Snipe through the heart.

'Tis now my sad task to relate
The wretched plight—the sorry state—
To which poor Snipe, who always used
To be efficient, was reduced
By two bright eyes and love's young dream.
His buttons lost their wonted gleam,
He started taking patent tonics:
He tuned transmitters to harmonics:
He referred to radar as RDF
And to correction seemed quite deaf.
He walked around in a sort of daze
And quite lost touch with AMOs.

In fact had Gert not stopped the rot,
The Section would have gone to pot.

One day he went to supervise
The carrying out of some 'DI's
When—Gertrude passing through the hangar—
He seemed to wake up from his langour
And tried to seize her by the arm—
Gertrude fled in some alarm:
With pounding heart and senses whirling,
She ran and hid behind a Stirling,
Upsetting in her headlong panic
A ladder supporting a flight mechanic.
But Snipe meanwhile had given chase
And seized her in a fierce embrace
With eyes aswim and knees all trembly
He kissed her by the tail assembly.
But Gertrude also could play rough.
She cried aloud, 'Oh Sir, enough.
You really are an awful pester.'
And she smacked him down with a bonding tester.
Was Snipe dismayed by this rebuff?
No, he was made of Sterner Stuff.

He continued daily so to plead
That Gert eventually agreed
To settle down and be his wife
And work his call signs out for life.
Gertrude indeed was nothing loth
That they should forthwith plight their troth
For she herself had quite a pash
For that lovely long black curled moustache.

Before we go we must not miss
A scene of perfect wedded bliss.
A winter's evening at half past eight:
A roaring fire burns in the grate:
Before it sit the happy pair—
Snipe in his favourite armchair,
With Group Officer Gertrude curled up at his feet,
While now and then as a special treat
She reads aloud a page or two—
From her AP.1762.

# Air Marshals' Anecdotes

The time: December 1978. The place: MoD London. The job: DGT—or, in plain English, Director General of RAF Training.

I undertook to stand in for the Air Member for Personnel at a British Legion dinner dance, his lady, I seem to recall, having met with a minor but incapacitating household accident shortly before the event. It was an important function in that the British Legion branch involved had consistently topped the fund-raising league for several years and their request for a senior serving officer and his wife at their major annual event clearly merited support. I only hoped that the unavoidable demotion of their guest of honour from Air Chief Marshal to Air Vice Marshal wouldn't spoil their fun or blunt their enthusiasm for raising cash!

I was living in a block of flats in Bloomsbury at the time and I asked my private secretary to arrange a pick-up there by a car from the Uxbridge MT section at 6.15 PM. The function was to take place at Epping and we were required to be there by 7.30 sharp. In due course my PS confirmed all systems 'go' for the evening but mentioned en passant that the driver was new to his job, having just been posted in from Saxa Vord or somewhere equally remote. Anyway, I was assured, the driver had undertaken to recce the route during the afternoon so that there would be no problems either with pick-up or timely travel thereafter to the ensuing revels.

The evening was a wet one with a gusty, chilling wind whipping up traffic spray from a steady torrential downpour, all of which was clearly discernable from the sitting-room window, where by 6.10 I was scanning the busy street below for the arrival of the Uxbridge vehicle. The minutes passed: 6.30 and then 6.45 came and went. At 7 PM there was still no car although a telephone call to Uxbridge had confirmed that it was en route. A few minutes later my wife and I quit the apartment to take up station in the foyer down below so that we would be poised to leap into the car the moment it arrived. It was obvious that we were going to be very late and in desperation, seething with impatience and not a little irritation, I left my wife in the lobby and stepped outside to peer anxiously up and down the street for any sign of the vehicle.

I wouldn't recommend standing on a wet and distinctly draughty street in central London at any time, but on a cold December evening, dressed in bum-freezer mess kit, amply bedecked in gold braid, beribboned with miniature medals, sporting a neck decoration at the collar, and finally topped off, so to speak, with an SD cap peaked with the generous ration of regulation air rank scrambled egg, you'd have to be a pretty remarkable person not to feel awkwardly conspicuous, self-conscious and somewhat over-dressed and out-of-place, let alone uncomfortably cold and wet. From the scant cover provided by a canopy over the entrance to the block, I tried to conceal my discomfort from passers-by whilst darting a look this way and that for a glimpse of the car. There was still no sign of it and by now I was very cross. The driver, if he ever did arrive, was going to get a tongue lashing he wouldn't forget, and if I had anything to do with his future, he'd be on his way back to Saxa for a repeat tour before the week was out.

I was brought back down to earth by a passing Indian or Pakistani. 'Excuse me, please, Mr Commissionaire,' he said with the utmost civility. 'Can you be telling me if we are doing bed and breakfast in this place?'

It just wasn't my night. The evening went from bad to worse but the rest is for telling another time.

Air Chief Marshal Sir Michael Beavis KCB CBE AFC

In 1951 I was posted on to No 41 Course at the Staff College, Bracknell. My DS on arrival was that fine officer Wing Commander, now Air Chief Marshal, Sir Christopher Foxley-Norris. He had, and still has, a great sense of fun and was adept at taking the mickey. I had been on the receiving end of this once or twice and decided that I would try and get my own back.

The opportunity arrived later in the course when he was on the stage in the lecture hall, conducting an exercise on the Middle East. Half-way through he turned to the audience and asked the rhetorical question, 'And where shall I put the aircraft carrier?'

I was on my feet in a flash. 'If I were you, sir,' I said, 'I would stuff it straight up the Shat-el-Arab.'

This brought the house down. Foxley-Norris looked none too pleased for a moment, but in the end he joined in the laughter and, I am happy to say, I went on to complete the course in reasonable order.

Air Chief Marshal Sir Derek Hodgkinson KCB CBE DFC AFC

At a flying training school in the early 1960s a foreign student with very recently acquired knowledge of English was on his Jet Provost night solo. He encountered an undercarriage problem of two greens and a red on his final circuit. Advice from the duty officer in the control tower failed to resolve the problem and, in due course, the Wing Commander Flying gave further instructions, but to no avail, apart from obvious rising panic in the cockpit. It was thought appropriate to bring in the Station Commander, who radioed personally, 'Five Three, this is the Station Commander. What is your endurance?' Complete silence ensued. The message was repeated several times with increasing severity of tone until eventually a quavering voice replied, 'The Prudential, sir!'

Air Chief Marshal Sir Douglas Lowe CBE DFC AFC

A station commander was giving a lunch to some worthy local ladies and briefed his steward not to fill the glass of the guest on his immediate right as she didn't approve of alcohol. After the second course she asked why her glass was unfilled.

'But aren't you the President of the Teetotal Society?'

'Oh no, Group Captain, I run the League of Purity.'

'Ah,' he said, 'I knew there was something you didn't do!'

Air Chief Marshal Sir Neville Stack KCB CVO CBE AFC

In 1947 I was the Wing Commander Flying at Changi in Singapore. We had on the airfield three squadrons of Dakotas and a communications squadron. The latter squadron had a variety of aircraft ranging from the Commander-in-Chief's York to the odd Auster for staff officers to get around Malaya. Both Air Command Far East and RAF Malaya had their HQ at Changi, so there were plenty of staff officers to use the aircraft.

One day two staff officers from RAF Malaya asked if they might take an Auster to Kuala Lumpur the next day and probably stay the night there. I agreed but pointed out that they would have to refuel each way at Kluang, that there were no RAF to look after them at Kluang, but that an army detachment there would refuel them from cans. They did not seem too happy at that prospect but accepted the situation.

Both of the staff officers were friends of mine, one a wing commander and one a squadron leader, and both were very experienced and much-decorated pilots. On their return, they were honest enough to tell us what had happened at Kluang on the outward journey.

They had duly landed at Kluang and taxied up to the refuelling point. The actual refuelling took place without incident but, of course, with no RAF ground crew to look after them, they had to start up on their own. The wing commander sat at the controls in the cockpit and the squadron leader, quite a big chap, started to swing the propeller. Apart from an occasional backfire, the engine simply would not start. In the middle of the morning in Malaya the squadron leader rapidly became exhausted, extremely hot and cross.

Whilst all this had been going on, there had been a soldier in jungle green, hat on the back of his head, leaning against a tree and watching it all with apparent curiosity. Whilst the poor squadron leader was resting, he sauntered over and said very casually, 'Excuse me, sir.'

He got no further before the squadron leader said, 'F— off, can't you see I'm busy.'

Fortunately, the soldier was not to be put off so easily and continued: 'I often watch these little aircraft visit here and I think they normally turn the propeller the other way.'

The squadron leader was dumbfounded, but without a word, tried the other way. The engine fired instantly and our two experienced wartime pilots got away as quickly as they could.

Air Chief Marshal Sir Neil Wheeler GCB CBE DSO DFC AFC

My wife often accompanied me on flying visits to stations in No 11 Group but did not do so on this particular visit to Leuchars. During my tour of the station, an airman came and told the Wing Commander Flying and my ADC (unbeknown to me) that my wife was about to land. The Wing Commander and my ADC went to the airfield and met my aircraft—but there was no AOC's wife aboard. Determined to track down the source of the false message the Wing Commander asked the airman, 'Who told you the AOC's wife was about to land?'

'Air Traffic Control, sir,' replied the airman.

'What exactly did they say?' persisted the Wing Commander, to which a now thoroughly unhappy airman replied, 'They said the AOC's bird was about to land.'

Air Marshal Sir Ivor Broom KCB CBE DSO DFC AFC

I was a young pilot officer at the Marine Aircraft Experimental Establishment at Felixstowe in 1927 and I was carrying out the duties of Orderly Officer—the first one on my own (i.e. not under instruction). I was very keen and no doubt full of my own importance, as I was well turned out in my No 1 Dress.

I entered the cookhouse and did not like the look of the floor, so I asked the airman on duty: 'Has the floor been mopped out this morning?'

To my surprise he just said: 'No.'

I was greatly put out by what I took to be a somewhat surly reply and I promptly said: 'No what?'

He merely replied, 'NO MOP!!'

For the moment, this most unexpected reply startled me but I suddenly remembered the advice I had been given by the OC Admin Flight, an ex-warrant officer, who had warned me to be on the lookout for carefully laid plots for the young pilot officers by some of the old hands. And in the cookhouse I soon discovered, of course, that he had plenty of mops if he had cared to look.

Air Marshal Sir Edward Chilton KBE CB

Amazing to realize that, when some of us joined the Service, there was a king on the throne: but the crowns on our earliest cap badges proved the point.

In those days, too, mess etiquette was very strictly observed, particularly at the flying training schools, where acting pilot officers were treated as the lowly beings they assuredly were—until the speeches, that is; and the rather alarming pursuits that followed them.

But the period up to the loyal toast was fairly well controlled—from time to time. At each (weekly) Guest Night or Dining-In, one of the brand-new APOs would be fingered as 'Mr Vice'—and would thereby automatically become the target for his colleagues. One of our number, slightly more responsible than the rest, took his duties very seriously indeed. For at least two days before the dinner, he could be heard muttering to himself: 'Gentlemen, The King'—until one felt that even he could remember it (I believe he later became a navigator).

On the evening in question, his dreaded mates decided to 'fix' the poor unfortunate. Only sherry was then allowed before dinner; but the barman was primed to ensure that certain other liquids became accidentally mixed therewith. And, by the dinner itself, our young friend was almost beyond recall. During dinner he rallied, with a great effort of will, to the point at which he could just recognize the call, 'Mr Vice, The King', and rise to his feet—but that was his limit. Raising his glass, he delivered himself of the immortal line: 'Kinglemen, the Gent'—and slipped quietly to the floor.

Air Chief Marshal Sir Michael Knight KCB AFC BA D LITT FRAeS

Back in the 1940s, while coming in to land at Coleby Grange in an Oxford, another Oxford doing the same thing flew into my back end. It was before the days of universal R/T and control was by Aldis lamp. It was pouring with rain and through the blurred windscreen both of us had got what each thought was a steady green 'Clear to land'. This was, in fact, far from so, but the first I knew of the aircraft was when its port propeller noisily chewed into my rear fuselage and neatly amputated my tailplane. Aeroplanes do not fly in this condition and, without really knowing what was happening, the next thing I clearly remember was slithering along the ground shedding bits of wing, fuselage and other parts.

Fortunately, we had been only about 50 feet up when the collision occurred and, even more fortunately, I was properly strapped in. Eventually, the noise of things breaking up stopped but by then I was left sitting in my seat clutching a useless control column and very little else around me. Extracting myself from the bits I got clear in time to see a staff car roaring across the airfield with the Station Commander's pennant fluttering from the bonnet. Never having met this great man, I thought I ought to show a proper degree of respect so, as he drew up, I threw him the best salute I could manage and cheerfully announced, 'It's all right, sir, no damage done,' meaning that I was personally unhurt.

Looking over his shoulder at the trail of wreckage strewn across several hundred yards of his airfield, his reply was a laconic, 'It . . . . . looks like it.'

With that he wound up his window and drove off, leaving me pondering on the ways of the mighty.

Air Vice-Marshal N. E. Hoad CVO CBE AFC

During Lord Louis Mountbatten's visit to the Royal Air Force Staff College at Andover in 1964 to deliver his address as Chief of the Defence Staff, I happened to notice that the very last of the most impressive array of medal ribbons adorning his chest resembled that of the Polish Air Force medal. (I should explain that a similar ribbon ended my own, much more modest, single row!)

Intrigued as to how he came to wear this somewhat unusual decoration, and emboldened by a couple of pre-lunch gin and tonics, I asked him at an opportune moment whether our respective ribbons were of the same decoration. Lord Mountbatten lifted his chest full of ribbons with his hand, looked down at them for a while, and said, 'To tell you the truth, old boy, I do not know what any of the ribbons in the last two rows are!'

Unbeknown to us, we were being photographed during this brief exchange by the College photographer, and to this day I treasure the photograph of the two of us—he looking down at his ribbons and I roaring with laughter—as a record of what must have been one of Lord Mountbatten's very rare admissions of ignorance!

Air Vice-Marshal A. Maisner CB CBE AFC

During the war, a flight lieutenant in the Royal Air Force got fed up with always being on readiness and having to rush out to his Spitfire, strap in and then never to get airborne. He decided, therefore, to train up a Chimpanzee to do his readiness—to dress up in flying kit and, when the siren went, to rush out to his Spitfire, put on his helmet, strap in and entirely represent the flight lieutenant until the 'all clear' sounded.

However, one day the alert was for real and the Chimpanzee had to take-off in his Spitfire and, believe it or not, he carried out a perfect interception against the Germans, shot down a ME 109 and then returned to base successfully. Now today that flight lieutenant is still a flight lieutenant and that Chimpanzee is a god damn Air Vice-Marshal in the Royal Air Force.

Air Vice-Marshal H. Bird-Wilson CBE DSO DFC AFC

In February 1942 I sailed, along with seven thousand other RAF cadets, across the Atlantic in what had been an old banana boat, the SS *Barfora*, to do my flying training in the USA.

The food on board was indescribably bad and living conditions in the hold were rather like the Black Hole of Calcutta. On the third day out one of my fellow cadets, an ex-graduate staff corporal who had survived the Dunkirk evacuation and was up to every scrounge, told me in a whisper that we could get a hot apple pie from the back of the cookhouse at 2 PM for half a crown (a goodly sum in those days and a significant proportion of our daily pay). The pie was delicious and well worth the money in my state of ravenous hunger.

Next day and the day after I again paid over my half-crown for a pie but by then a large queue had begun to form round the deck and inevitably attracted the attention of the Captain.

There were no more apple pies for the remaining four days on board and the food remained as bad as ever. Justice may have been done but I wish it could have awaited the end of the crossing, for the cook, who had been running a profitable racket with the ship's provisions, was placed under arrest.

Marshal of the Royal Air Force, Sir Michael Beetham GCB CBE DFC AFC FRAeS

I was presenting prizes once at a School Speech Day, and the Headmaster, who had dutifully looked me up in *Who's Who*, gave a rather lengthy list of all my previous appointments and the dates when he introduced me to the assembled parents and their offspring. The prizes having been duly handed over, I mingled with the crowd at the tea tent. As I was waiting for my cup of tea I overheard one parent saying to another: 'Was that chap who presented the prizes any good? From what the Headmaster said about him I gathered that he'd never held any of his jobs for more than a year or two.'

Marshal of the Royal Air Force Sir David Craig GCB OBE MA FRAeS RAF

No 611 Squadron was based at Redhill as part of the Kenley Wing, flying Spitfire Mk Vs in May/June 1942. One beautiful summer morning, the Commanding Officer, Squadron Leader Douglas Watkins DFC R AUX AF, did an air test on his aircraft from which he made a particularly good three-point landing. Upon entry to the squadron crew room, a bright and bushy-tailed young pilot officer said, 'Oh sir! what a very good landing.'

Watkins's rather sardonic reply was, 'Mmm! I didn't know I was down until I heard the groundcrew clapping.'

Air Chief Marshal Sir John Aitken KCB

**An Allied Victory**

In September 1944 No 133 (Norwegian) Wing moved to Grimbergen, a small grass airfield some 3 or 4 miles north of Brussels. The only other occupants of the airfield were three coveys of partridges, which spent all the time in the middle of the field and as such were a constant threat to Spitfires landing and taking off, particularly the latter.

The partridges were far too alert to allow anyone to get close enough to have a shot at them, and ignored all our attempts to persuade them to leave the field. In desperation, I decided to try a new tactic. I would drive the Humber utility car and Lieutenant Colonel Berg, the Wing Leader, would be my passenger, armed with the Wing's skeet-shooting shot gun and its practice ammunition. To enable us to get close enough for a kill with this weak ammunition we would have to get very close to the coveys.

On the first run the coveys were flushed when we were 40 to 50 yards away, and flew down the field for 400 yards approx. We followed at full speed, flushed the birds again, and this time they only flew for about 200 yards. Twice more we flushed and followed them, until they were so exhausted they could no longer get airborne and we were able to catch a number by hand. They made a welcome change to our menus.

The Wing left shortly afterwards to an airfield in Holland without any bird accidents to aircraft. There was, however, an interesting sequel when on 1 January 1945, the *Luftwaffe* carried out its wide-ranging and final mass attack on the Allied airfields. In the official report on this attack, which I read some months later, was the report of a ME 109 aircraft which had forced-landed just outside Grimbergen airfield. It appeared that the pilot had already straffed the major Allied airfield of Melsbrook, a few miles away, and then over-flew Grimbergen, where were assembled a large number of Allied bombers which had forced-landed. The ME 109 went into an attack and at the bottom of his dive, collected a partridge in his air intake, and as a result crash landed in a field nearby.

A victory for the partridges in retaliation for the disturbance we had caused them.

Air Marshal Sir Douglas Morris KCB CBE DSO DFC

Whilst serving in Gibraltar in the early 1970s, I was invited from time to time to give the address in one or other of the local churches; so also were my Naval and Military counterparts.

On one occasion, in St Andrews Church and because it was Whitsun, I had chosen as my text that verse from *Acts* that reads: 'And they were all amazed and looked at one another saying, what does this mean.'

I then went on to argue that the Apostles, at Pentecost, did perhaps not speak with many tongues but instead, sensing a great occasion, heard what they wanted to hear.

No sooner had I voiced this far from original heresy than the senior Scottish lady in Gibraltar rose to her feet and walked out of the church. Since she was a much-respected and much-loved individual, I was distinctly uncomfortable.

She telephoned later in the day—to apologize. Something I had said had provided the answer to a clue in the previous day's *Times* crossword—and she had gone home to fill it in before she forgot.

Air Marshal Sir Charles Ness KCB CBE CBIM MIPM

During the 1939–45 war, I was Station Commander, Linton-on-Ouse. A Halifax returned from a raid with a bomb which hadn't released for some reason, but which fell off near Harrogate. As it was one of the new big bombs designed by the Armament Staff, they rushed up to see the enormous damage it must have caused.

They interviewed a farmer who, working near to where the bomb fell, commented, 'Eeh, it moost, 'ave been a big 'un, it blew me bloody 'at off.'

Collapse of the Armament Staff.

Air Marshal Sir John Whitley KBE CB DSO AFC

I remember one Dining-in-Night speech in which—when feeling untypically serious (and perhaps a trifle pompous)—I compared the role of the Station Commander to that of an orchestral conductor.

The Flying Wing (or Ops Wing) were the strings, providing the main theme, soaring to their climaxes in strong unison. The Engineering Wing provided the brass and percussion, big, bold and brash. The Administrative Wing were the woodwind, making their essential if somewhat plaintive contribution.

The music they played was scored for the whole orchestra and not for just one section of it. The tempo was seldom *andante*, usually *allegro*, sometimes *con fuoco*.

The conductor was there to draw from all the players their best performances. Certainly he did not claim to be able to play all the instruments in the orchestra. But he did have to know the score.

Air Vice-Marshal D. J. Furner CBE DFC AFC

In December 1944, when it looked as though the war was in its final stages, there tended to be a certain amount of joyriding between airfields on the Continent and the UK. An Air Ministry Order was issued expressly forbidding such flights except with high-level authorization. However, the dashing Station Commander of an airfield in Belgium, wishing to give his troops a treat on Christmas Day, arranged for a Dakota to 'get lost' and to land in Northern Ireland to refuel, accidentally picking up a load of turkeys. Alas! The flight was detected and the CO soon received one of those letters beginning:

> Sir, I am directed by the Air Council to draw your attention to the flight of Dakota **so and so** on December 19th and to AMO **so and so** . . . Please explain forthwith.

The reply was masterly.

> Sir,
>
> I have the honour to acknowledge receipt of your letter—and to draw your attention to another Air Ministry Order, number—, which emphasized the duty of all ranks to do everything possible to mitigate the shortage of personnel at this critical stage of the war, and in particular to ensure the security of airfields and other bases by every means possible.
>
> Being aware of the risk to my very lightly defended airfield, I sought other means of providing better security without asking for increased guards. I thought myself of the geese which were used to give the alarm in ancient Rome. Unfortunately, I was unable to find any geese, but with the assistance of a helpful colleague I located some turkeys and the Dakota in question was despatched to collect them. The turkeys were duly placed on a watch-keeping roster at points around the airfield. Copies of my relevant SRO's are attached.
>
> Unfortunately, after some three or four days it became evident that more manpower was used in feeding the turkeys, putting them on watch and returning them to their accommodation than saved by using their watch-keeping qualities. So on December 25th, in order to avoid any loss to non-public funds, the turkeys were reduced to produce.

A good try but alas 'their airships' were not amused.

Air Vice-Marshal W. E. Oulton CB CBE DSO DFC

# Other Anecdotes

## RAF Melbourne, Yorks, 1944

An air commodore was visiting No 10 Squadron and it was arranged that he would join the flight deck of a Halifax on an air test. The skipper told Sergeant Smith to escort the visiting officer to the parachute section to be fitted out with a parachute harness for the trip. The air commodore was dressed in an Irving flying jacket, without hat, and therefore without obvious evidence of his rank.

On completion of the kitting out, he was required to fill in the appropriate form with his number, rank and name. Unfortunately, there was insufficient space for him to write his full rank so he abbreviated it to AC. The airman behind the counter inspected the entry and asked: 'Is that AC 1 or AC 2?'

The astonished senior officer replied: 'Air Commodore, you idiot.'

'Oh yeah,' said the airman, 'that'll be the day, that will.'

Sergeant 'Bill' Smith

## RAF Marston Moor, 1944

This unit was the home of the Whitley bomber conversion course and the transitory aircrew, who had a reputation for high spirits but low morals.

The Queen Bee (the senior WAAF officer) was lecturing a group of newly arrived WAAFs on the need to beware of the attention of the evil aircrew. One particular girl, obviously keen but dim, pointed her finger to her head and said: 'Don't worry, ma'am, I've got it up here!'

'I don't care where you've got it, my dear!' replied the Queen Bee, 'they'll bloody well find it.'

## Hastings OCU, RAF Dishforth, Early 1960s

A rather dour and 'much-held-in-awe' Polish Instrument Rating Examiner (IRE), walking back to the crew-room with a new young co-pilot (NYC) who had just flown his first rating trip on Hastings.

IRE: 'Well, my boy, what you think of trip, eh?'

NYC: 'Not too bad, sir.'

IRE: 'No need to call me sir—this is OCU now, not flyink school. Tell, me what your mother call you?'

NYC: (Thinking things are looking good) 'Peter.'

IRE: 'Well, Peter, you failed!'

Flight Lieutenant C. L. Green

## Stalag Luft III, 1944

Having thoroughly exhausted the patience of the German Camp Commandant and the guards, Wing Commander Douglas Bader locked himself in his barrack room and refused to comply with the various orders and entreaties to give himself up to the authorities for whatever punishment he had incurred for his many escapades and gibes at the Goons in general.

An armed escort of some twenty fully armed guards in combat gear under the command of a very precise and fearsome looking SS major marched into the camp. Bader was persuaded by the Senior British Officer, and his friends, to give himself up and duly appeared to be escorted by the guards to the punishment cells. The guards were brought smartly to attention and given the order 'Right turn', preparatory to marching away with Bader. Every guard complied, with the exception of one poor lad, who, in front of some 1,000 cheering and jeering Kriegies, turned *left*. Chaos reigned for some minutes, with Bader milking the situation to the limits, and eventually giving the order to march off, himself at the head.

Wing Commander L. A. E. Osbon

## Moascar Astra, 1953

In 1953 I was stationed at the Army Education Centre in Moascar in the Suez Canal Zone. Much of our work was with National Servicemen. One of the facilities which we enjoyed most was the open-air cinema run by the Royal Air Force and—naturally—known as the Astra. In an examination paper, an RAF National Serviceman translated PER ARDUA AD ASTRA as 'After Work to the Cinema'.

Major R. Francis

## RAF Bishops Court, 1962

A group of RAF and civil air traffic controllers at Ulster Radar were busy playing crib, waiting for the evening's flying programme to start. In the background, the weather and atmospheric conditions were causing a lot of crackling and interference on the radio loudspeaker. Suddenly an airliner called up: 'Ulster Radar, this is Speedbird 623, we're getting a lot of interference on this frequency. Can you hear church organ music?'

A controller leapt to his feet, grabbed the microphone and replied: 'Speedbird 623, negative, but I can offer you a lower flight level.'

## RAF College, Cranwell, Early 1960s

Junior Flight Cadets (JFC) were required, in their first year, to broaden their outlook by making several visits to Industrial Plants, etc., including a trip to a Nottingham coal mine. JFCs were also required to do as bid by Senior Flight Cadets (SFC).

One Wednesday afternoon, a JFC returned from a mine visit, had his shower and was walking out of college in blazer and flannels when a SFC called out: 'Go fetch my golf clubs, please, and bring them to my car.'

Shortly afterwards, the JFC was on his way out, golf bag on shoulder, when he passed the commandant, who enquired: 'Good afternoon, Wilks. Been playing golf, I see?'

JFC, without thinking, replied, 'No, Sir, I've been down a coal mine.'

Flight Lieutenant C. L. Green

## Food Poisoning

In 1987 one of our No 101 Squadron co-pilots happened to be flying the day before he was due to go away to his wedding. As they returned to Brize Norton, his Captain said that he wasn't feeling very well and that the co-pilot would have to fly the approach and landing as well as arranging for an ambulance to meet them after landing. This our hero duly did; however, what he didn't know was that Air Traffic Control, the medical centre and various others had been tipped off that this was a complete hoax.

The crew was taken to the medical centre, where various 'tests' were carried out. As soon as the co-pilot went in for his tests, the rest of the crew made their escape back to the ambulance, having been 'cleared', the captain having been kept in for observation for 'suspected food poisoning'.

Once the co-pilot had returned to the squadron, the medical centre called him urgently, saying that they had found something irregular with his tests and that he'd better not go anywhere until certain arrangements were made. The poor lad had a miserable few hours waiting for news and eventually the medical centre rang to tell him that they were sending an ambulance to take him direct to the officers' mess to pick up his things before they rushed him off to Wroughton Hospital for an emergency operation. He was duly bundled into the ambulance and taken to the mess—whereupon he was taken straight to the bar and let off the hook by his friends and the captain, who had made the quickest recovery from food poisoning known to medical science!

Flight Lieutenant N. J. Wilcock

# Cast Not Thy Bread upon the Waters

The less staid among us may recall the comic football matches, a Service institution at Christmas; indeed they might still flourish. One such moment (tropical madness?) took place at RAF China Bay, Trincomalee, Ceylon, on Christmas Day 1940. The war, as yet, was ocean(s) away. The performance of one contender gave this event particular sparkle.

Our hero was the reigning Station Warrant Officer, Chairman and Treasurer of the Sergeants' Mess Committee, 'popular' martinet and, nearing the half century, still a keen footballer. As Captain of the NCOs and airmen, he appeared a little late, clad in sarong and Bombay bowler with chinstrap. Apart from an early contretemps with the referee (the Station Commander) regarding the sun's direction, the SWO (hereinafter Chiefy) led his side to victory over the officers, 5–0; this in spite of an inclination to disappear occasionally in the direction of the Flight Offices.

Mayhem over, the contingent, minus Station Commander, Orderly Officer and Orderly Sergeant, set a fast reciprocal course for the seaplane slipway at the Bay end and took the plunge in unison. There was some recollection that Chiefy did the same, less sarong, khaki shirt tail in full flow, yet still bowlered. Thereafter, he was not conspicuous. Yet, refreshed, our other heroes returned to the slipway and McEwans Export assembled at the ready. Then, a keen observer (GD Nav) focussed on a steady stream of paper, bobbing gently, wind assisted, Indian-Ocean bound. Then someone screamed, 'MONEY! MONEY'! There followed a sortie of squadron swimmers in a sweep and hunt to exhaustion. They emerged clutching wads of rupee notes. At this stage Chiefy was sighted, in the buff apart from wristband coat of arms. He was also in a dinghy and slept seraphically.

There had to be a connection, and there was. It appeared that Chiefy closed the mess bar at 0100 on Christmas Day, then tottered to his room, complete with bar takings, in shorts and shirt. The sole witness, our number one Sinhalese mess waiter, corroborated this at the hastily assembled quayside Board of Inquiry. He had attached no importance to the matter. The officers at the quayside did and sensibly abstained from the Inquiry. Ashen-faced (pension in mind), Chiefy balanced the books, alfresco, with the aid of a whip round to cover one or two 'floating losses'. A shattered clutch of officers and NCOs served the airmen's Christmas Dinner two hours late. Chiefy (God Bless him) was not in evidence.

The postscript to this pantomime was that, for some days a moratorium seemed to be declared on misdemeanours in or about the mess and other places within Chiefy's purview. Eventually life and his clinical efficiency returned to normal. It was said that the CO was never privy to the story. Or was he?

Squadron Leader E. I. Williams

## No 1 Radio School, RAF Cranwell, 1947

Few aircraft apprentices passed out from training without having been awarded a period of 'Jankers'. Evening cookhouse fatigues were a virtually inescapable feature of Jankers but, as a means of access to food, had a certain degree of compensation. The RAF kitchen was supervised by a particularly well-endowed WAAF flight sergeant who observed an apprentice dip his mug into a churn of milk.

'Apprentice!' she called out, 'You can't drink that—it's WAAFs' milk.' (Being girls, WAAFs had extra rations.)

Chastened, the apprentice replied: 'Sorry, Flight Sergeant, but I didn't know and it *tasted* just like cows' milk to me!'

## RAF Colerne, 1942

Breakfast used to be served in a walled-off corner of the hangar and for weeks it was always sausages—dreadful they were!

Some of the lads had returned from detachment and brought with them a 'trophy' won from outside a chapel. It was a poster and was duly fixed to the door of the cook-house.

It read:

Jesus Christ
The same yesterday
The same today
The same evermore'

## One-way Trip

It was 24 November 1977; I was doing my categorization on the Puma at Odiham, near the M3 in Hampshire. They were lean years, with frozen pay and defence-spending cuts. On the penultimate sortie under the beady eye of Squadron Leader Duncan Donaldson, there were indications of transmission failure. I thought Duncan was testing me out. He always liked to catch out senior officers. We were perfectly placed; he had obviously planned it. So I calmly put us down in a field near the M3. He then told me it had been for real—but I was doing fine so he did not interfere.

To repair the helicopter in the field was too complicated. They decided to take it home. So they folded back the blades, towed it onto the M3 and back to Odiham. Off the M3 coming through Odiham village a massive tail-back resulted. The car drivers were very patient. You don't often see a Puma helicopter being towed up the road.

A driver shouted to the NCO walking behind the helicopter, 'What's up, Sarge?' Back came the reply. 'It's the defence cuts, sir—we can only afford to fly one way.'

Air Commodore D. Allison CBE

## Oranges and Chocolates

In September 1942 I was flying Whitleys from Stornoway in the Hebrides with No 58 Squadron, searching the Atlantic for U-boats. We took off just before dawn, carrying four depth charges and the usual supply of scarce oranges and chocolate. At about 1,000 feet, the engines stopped. Whilst the two pilots were busy finding a spot on the shore to glide to, I kept the crew in the rear informed of what was happening. In spite of being badly burned and crawling away from a burning plane containing depth charges (they did not explode), I had to laugh when the boys in the back told me they had managed to eat all the oranges and chocolate before we hit the ground. There must be a moral in that somewhere.

Sergeant G. Garside

## RAF Halton, 1939

The Wing Warrant Officer at RAF Halton detailed an aircraft apprentice to water the sergeants' mess garden, so the apprentice got a watering can and started to water, but it began to pour with rain so he said, 'Blow this,' or words to that effect and went to the Naafi for a char and a wad.

Later on, the Warrant Officer saw the apprentice and said, 'I thought I told you to water the garden?'

'Yes,' the apprentice said, 'but it was raining, sir.'

'Well!' said the WO, 'you've been issued with a ground sheet,* haven't you?'

(**used as a cape pre-war*)

## RAF St Mawgan, 1962

One Saturday morning parade, an airman was seen to be wearing black brothel creepers with thick black soles.

The inspecting officer asked: 'Are those your best shoes?'

'No, sir.'

'Then why are you not wearing your best shoes?'

'Please, sir, because my best shoes are brown.'

## RAF Linton-on-Ouse, 1959

During daytime local flying practice a student pilot decided to 'beat up' a steam train heading north from York. To the surprise of the pilot, the train crew reacted, with the fireman hurling lumps of coal at the piston-engined Provost, one scoring a direct hit. The next morning, the Flight Commander summoned the student, who vigorously denied low flying but could not explain how the coal fragments jammed between the cylinder barrels had got there!

## RAF Bruggen, 1984

Prior to the inspection of the station by a Very Senior Officer (VSO), the airmen of one of the squadrons were being pre-briefed and were instructed: 'If the Inspecting Officer speaks to you, be honest and speak clearly!'

During the inspection the VSO stopped and spoke to one of the Corporals.

VSO: 'What do you do, Corporal?'

Cpl: 'Not a lot, sir.'

VSO: 'Oh, why not?'

Cpl: 'Well, sir, I'm an Air Radar Fitter awaiting the arrival of Tornados. At present my squadron has Jaguars with no airborne radar, so there is not much for me to do.'

VSO: 'Good answer, Corporal. Keep up the good work.'

The Very Senior Officer then turned to the airman standing next in line: 'And what do *you* do?'

Airman: 'I help him.'

## PM RAF Hospital, Halton, 1950

A Sister passing the bed of a young American airman enquired where he was from. 'High Wycombe, ma'am,' he replied.

Apart from his pronunciation, the term ma'am was unfamiliar to her ears and she wasn't sure she liked it. 'Would you mind very much,' she asked, 'not calling me ma'am. Please call me Sister.'

The poor lad was overcome with confusion. 'Gee, ma'am,' he said, 'I couldn't do that. Back home that's familiar.'

## Primitive Approach Aids

In the early 1950s HQ No 18 Group, Coastal Command, was at Pitreavie Castle, and its communications flight operated from Leuchars. One of the regular trips was from Leuchars to Donibristle to pick up Command Staff, and then fly to Kinloss.

Because of the numerous big lumps of stone that reach up into the sky in that part of Caledonia, it was always reassuring to fly in the clear bits, but unfortunately, to land at Kinloss, it was necessary on many occasions to descend through cloud to renew contact with terra firma.

During one particular trip, loaded up with a number of Group HQ Staff, the descent was made in the usual manner, i.e. watch the needles, reduce engine power, descend through cloud, etc.

Following the uneventful landing, one of the Command Staff, no doubt suitably impressed by the descent through the murk virtually on to the end of the runway, asked how it had been achieved. At the end of the explanation about tuning to the strong beacon at Burghead, the Staff Officer agreed that it was indeed 'a strong beacon, it could be heard in the passenger compartment'.

The signaller didn't have the heart (or was it something else?) to explain that the 'beacon' that had been heard at the back was in fact the very audible klaxon, warning that the engines were at a reduced power setting and that the undercarriage had not been lowered.

It must have been the right decision; shortly afterwards he was promoted to Master Signaller.

Corporal A. Hackett

## What Did We Do Wrong?

Late in 1940 our unit, No 14 WIS (Wireless Intelligence Screen), travelled from White Waltham to Penrhos in North Wales, with an overnight stop at RAF Bridgnorth. There, at Bridgnorth, I feel our attitude to polished floors and Initial Training Units may not have been all it should have been.

Several weeks later we were returning to White Waltham, with again an overnight stop at Bridgnorth, when our convoy of about eighteen vehicles and about 100 plus bods was stopped on the road outside Bridgnorth, and the word was passed back down the length of the convoy, 'They won't let us in.'

After some negotiations by our CO, it was agreed that we would be given a meal, the vehicles refuelled and we would proceed on our way. I can recall there was considerable German activity over the Midlands on that particular night; the fact that we were fed and refuelled would indicate there was no logistical problem—so why were we unwelcome?

By my reckoning this made us the only unit of RAF to have been refused entry to an RAF station.

Corporal D. W. Jones

## Gents

One day at the latter end of the war a certain Flight Sergeant Pilot (me) on No 150 Squadron (Lancasters) at Hemswell had bid his girl friend good night and was waiting for the train at Newark to return to Lincoln in time to catch the stage-coach back to Hemswell.

The local trains were 'compartment' coaches, and one always took precautions in the Gents, which I did. It was a very dark night, but being blessed with excellent night vision I was able to find the stalls without difficulty.

Not so the boozed-up erk who lurched in and let fly where he stopped—right down my right trouser leg!! Despite being somewhat upset, I was able to give him a fairly reasonable run-down of his predecessors and their most dubious legitimacy, which I think he was sufficiently able to appreciate.

I then stormed out of the Gents, shaking my leg in anger, and moved up the platform.

A few minutes later this bod poured himself out of the Gents and went to join his mates, laughing his head off. In a very boozy voice he then said, and I quote, 'Boys, I've just had the ambition of my lifetime. I've pissed over a Flight Sergeant!'

Flight Sergeant A. M. Dickson

## PM RAF Hospital Wroughton, 1969

Slightly doddery, very senior retired Air Chief Marshal speaking to Ward Sister:

ACM: 'I say, sistah, when does this jolly old eclipse of the moon come off?

Sister: 'Oh, it's not an eclipse, sir, its a moon landing.'

ACM: 'Don't talk bloody rubbish!!'

## RAF Andreas, Isle of Man, 1943

Breakfast time in the airmens' mess and the Orderly Sergeant was in attendance. A young airman (an erk) was enjoying his porridge until he reached the bottom of the plate and discovered, on the end of his spoon, a contraceptive (which had obviously been planted by a colleague).

The startled airman called over the Orderly Sergeant, who was equally bemused, and together they marched up to the servery. 'What's all this?' demanded the sergeant.

Without hesitation, the Corporal turned to one of his chefs and said: 'Take that one back and give him another one!'

## RAF Upwood, 1945

Some WAAFs were returning to their quarters after an evening's socializing down town. Unfortunately, it was 11.30 PM and they should have reported back by 10.30 PM. At the gatehouse they were cautioned by an RAF policeman: 'You're out after hours!'

'That makes a change,' replied one of the girls, 'you're normally out after ours.'

## RAF Upwood, 1948

Petrol was still rationed and as a result the camp was full for the weekend.

The Orderly Officer, escorted by the Orderly Sergeant, was carrying out his inspection of the dining hall, which was packed with airmen devouring their tea. The Orderly Officer was a large, humourless individual, feared by everyone.

At each table in turn the Orderly Sergeant asked: 'Any complaints?'

No one dared express a grievance until the very last table, when AC2 Plonk exclaimed: 'Yes please, Sarge, I've got a caterpillar on my salad.'

Pushing aside the sergeant, the Orderly Officer marched up to the airman, peered at the lettuce, said: 'What's wrong with that?', picked up the caterpillar and ate it.

Outside the mess the Orderly Officer turned to the sergeant and said: 'These bloody airmen complain about f— all nowadays.'

## RAF Scampton, 1948

The Air Officer Commanding (AOC) was expected for his annual formal inspection. During the previous year's visit the AOC had criticized the lack of toilet rolls in the barrack block WCs and consequently every effort was made this time to ensure that all cubicles were properly equipped.

The AOC, accompanied by his entourage, began his inspection and, as expected, paid special attention to the toilets. He marched from one to another, opening and closing doors until he reached a door that was locked. Realizing, in his wisdom, that the WC was occupied, he shouted through the door: 'Is there any paper in there?'

To which came the reply: 'Hang on, tosh, you can have some of this when I've finished.'

Sergeant 'Bill' Smith

## RAF Singapore, 1953

An airman was up before the subordinate commander for committing an offence. After hearing the evidence and being convinced of the guilt of the accused, the office announced: 'Fourteen days' restrictions for the offence and for calling me a bastard.'

'But, sir,' pleaded the airman, 'I didn't call you a bastard.'

'You will when you get outside, lad,' said the officer.

## RAF Coningsby, 1955

The Air Officer Commanding (AOC) was due to arrive to carry out his annual formal inspection. A large parade stood-at-ease in pouring rain and waited a considerable time for the AOC's delayed flight to land.

Eventually, much to the relief of the assembled ranks, he arrived and, accompanied by the station commander and Senior Warrant Officer (SWO), commenced his inspection.

As they passed a column of drenched airmen, a voice from the rear was heard to say: 'They also serve who stand and wait.'

'Who said that?' snapped the SWO.

'Milton, sir,' came the reply.

'Right, Milton', said the SWO, 'I'll deal with you later.'

## It's Your Funeral!!

It was Spring in 1940, I was stationed at No 9 SFTS Hullavington and whilst awaiting my aircrew course was attached to No 10 MU stores. A Flight

Lieutenant Mackenzie was in charge (i/c). I was due a long-weekend pass and in the traditional manner wondered if I could wangle an 'early pass'. Only one way to find out, ask the boss! Flight Lieutenant Mackenzie had signed my pass the day before, so he was aware that I would be off for the weekend. So it was that on that Friday morning I entered his office and asked if he would agree to signing an 'early pass' from that midday instead of waiting until early evening before I could proceed. He asked if all the various manuals were up to date and I assured him they were. He signed the pass and hoped I would have a pleasant weekend.

I had lunch, then made my way to the Guard Room to book out, feeling very elated. Having signed out, I made my way to the main gate, haversack and respirator over my shoulder, feeling on top of the world. Hullavington was designed like many other peacetime RAF stations, a treelined entrance for several hundred yards before coming to the main road. As I left the main gate behind me, the Station Band came round the far corner from the main road, followed by half a dozen or so airmen with rifles, and several others. The band was playing Colonel Bogey!

The rifle party and band passed by, then suddenly an arm shot out, grabbed me, and a harsh voice bawled, 'Get fell in behind.' It was Flight Sergeant Breeze NCO i/c Service Police. Imagine the scene, one moment I am proceeding on leave, as happy as a pig in you know what, the next I am 'fell in' behind the Station Band, marching the other way to Colonel Bogey. What foul deed had I committed? Which particular section of KRs had I breached? I hadn't a clue.

At the Guard Room the party was halted. The rifle party then moved off and others present dismissed. 'You, you 'orrible little man, get inside,' bawled Breeze. Once in the Guard Room he glared at me with all the wrath of the Gods. 'And where do you think you were going?' he demanded. 'On weekend pass,' I replied. 'Yer waz, but you can forget that,' he replied. Tongue in cheek, I nervously asked why. ''ow long 'ave you been in the Air Force?' he asked. I told him three months, to which his response was: 'That's long enough to know to stand to attention when a funeral party passes.' I was shattered. 'But, Flight Sergeant,' I stammered, 'the band was playing Colonel Bogey. How could I know it was a funeral party?' He pulled himself to his full height, face puce with rage. 'We was coming back,' he shouted, 'Get back to your billet.'

I returned to the Stores and when Flight Lieutenant Mackenzie saw me he said: 'Aren't you going to use the early pass I signed?' When I told him what had happened I thought he would fall off his chair laughing. He then picked up the telephone, rang the Main Guard Room and told Flight Sergeant Breeze I was to be allowed to proceed on pass. When booking out for the second time, Breeze put on his most grotesque expression, glared at me and spluttered, 'I'll get you yet.'

How right he was! A week later I was on a charge for walking on the grass and was given seven days' CB (confined to barracks).

Warrant Officer D. Kneale

## RAF Sutton-on-Hull, 1959

A group of sleepy air traffic controllers was listening to a lecture on first aid on a warm summer's afternoon. A young, enthusiastic Medical Officer was explaining the symptoms of shock and was describing in detail the effect on the eyes and the dilation of the pupils: 'Dilation is quite a common phenomenon,' said the MO. 'In fact, what would you expect to happen to my pupils if I closed my eyes?'

'We'd all f— off!' came the reply.

## RAF Heliopolis, Egypt, 1938

One Christmas Eve No 216 Squadron decorated the top floor (three storeys high) of the accommodation block as a Wild West Saloon and hired cowboy outfits, guns and blank ammunition. They couldn't get horses so instead hired six donkeys, which were lifted on the shoulders of a drunken 'wee' No 113 Squadron member up the three flights of stairs and deposited safely in the Saloon. Three days of festivities later, an illustrious visitor discovered both the airmen and donkeys were drunk, with one donkey lying on the floor and an airman fast asleep with his head on its stomach.

## Late Breakfast

21 February 1945 Lancaster JO-Z No 463 (RAAF) Squadron

Returning from Germany we had a difference of opinion with a night-fighter. Our entire crew survived after baling out over Holland.

Some forty years later, Squadron Leader Ray Leach was compiling the history of Waddington, and I was approached for photographs and memorabilia. In the course of a phone conversation, I mentioned to him that the RAF had owed me a flying breakfast for over forty years.

This no doubt amused him, for on our visit to 'Waddo', instead of the steak pie ordered at lunch I was served a full breakfast.

If nothing else, I feel I hold a record for being served with the latest breakfast ever served by the RAF—late by forty years.

Sergeant S. Bridgeman

## . . . Make That Two!

When once it was renowned as a Bomber Command
There was produced—upon demand—
For crews returning from the flak
An egg and bacon 'Welcome Back'.
It was intended by night-fighters—Hun—
That we should not enjoy such fun
And it was to our dismay
One caught us on our homeward way!
For forty years we nursed the thought
A flying breakfast that came to nought,
And then in nineteen eighty-five
Waddington's history we helped revive
The 'Blue Room' was the epic scene
And Strike Command
Served egg, bacon and beans
Our Flying Breakfast we did eat
Served by a waiter, oh so neat.
Our parody is ended
For I did not have the heart
To inform our host that
I'd eaten egg, bacon and beans
*Before* my journey's start.

## Stalag IVB 1943–5

'Gen' was the name of one of the hand-scripted wall magazines published in the RAF compound of the notorious Stalag IVB at Muhlberg. It was widely read amongst the 15,000 inmates.

The Red Cross parcels from Canada contained a powdered milk called 'KLIM' in a useful-sized tin. The tins were used by POWs for drinking, cooking and culinary purposes. Hence the pseudonym of the camp poet: RUDDYOT KLIMTIN.

In Kriegie parlance we were 'Muckers'. We shared the 'Slings and Arrows' in the nightmare existence of RAF Hut 43a and together we culled the few lighter facts of this crazy life. Through the medium of 'Gen' the world laughed with us—we wept alone.

On St George's Day 1945 the wires were down; Stalag IVB had been liberated by St George in somewhat soiled armour, represented by three Cossacks mounted on shaggy Mongol ponies. RUDDYOT KLIMTIN vanished into the sunset.

AC1 T. H. Valentine

## Low Flying, Pigs and The Sound Barrier

I served on the flying complaints flight at HQ P&SS UK at both Acton and Rudloe Manor. My task was to investigate complaints made by members of the public about aircraft noise. During the seven years, I heard many comments about the RAF and our American colleagues.

The funniest I thought was that from a farmer who bred pigs near the approach to Cowden range. The telephone rang. I picked the thing up and said cheerfully: 'HQ P&SS flying complaints, Flight Sergeant White speaking.'

A voice replied: You stop this b— awful flying, your rotten pilots have upset my pigs again, you are the one in charge of this, so you can stop it right now! If you don't, I'll take five tons of pig dung and place it in front of the gate to Cowden domestic area!'

I explained the training requirements of pilots etc. and he slammed the telephone down. Ten minutes later the farmer telephoned again and said: 'The flying hasn't stopped. I've dumped the pig dung on the approach road and I am sending you a bill of £20 for its delivery.'

Once again he slammed the telephone down. Later the range officer at Cowden telephoned to say that the farmer had in fact dumped the pig dung and the station range personnel were having to clear it. I didn't get the bill.

On another occasion, on a visit to a Welsh farming community, I gave a lecture on the requirements for aircrew to train to fly low. Following the lecture I asked a group of farmers which aircraft caused most disturbance. The farmers, who were taken aback, went into a rugby scrum huddle for a few moments. Then one stepped forward and said quite proudly, 'Now then, bach! the aircraft which cause most noise are the Sound Barriers.'

Sergeant J. White, RAF Policeman

## . . . That is the Question . . .

No 2 (Army Cooperation) Squadron and No 3 (Fighter) Squadron were formed from the same company of the Royal Engineers at Larkhill on 13 May 1912. Both are rightly proud of their common origin and their subsequent separate histories. There has always been great rivalry between them, each, of course, claiming to have been the first to fly heavier-than-air machines while No 1 Squadron was still equipped with balloons. Indeed, the motto of No 3 (F) Squadron is TERTIUS PRIMUS ERIT, 'The Third Shall Be First.' Both squadrons have been based in Germany since World War Two.

In the mid-1950s No 3 Squadron was at Geilenkirchen, flying Sabre 4s, and No 2 Squadron was at Wahn with Meteor FR9s. It was decided that No 3 Squadron should move to Geilenkirchen. The move was made while No 3

Squadron was detached to Sylt for an Armament Practice Camp. When they returned they found that on every available chalk board and perspex surface in their hangar and ops. room was written 'TERTIUS SECUNDUS ERIT'! But not long afterwards the laugh was to be on No 2 Squadron.

Their Meteors were to be replaced by Swift FR5s. So on one of the last occasions when they would have twelve serviceable Meteors, they decided to fly a figure '2' over the airfield. Easy: three fours; a finger four; an echelon; and a line abreast. Thus:

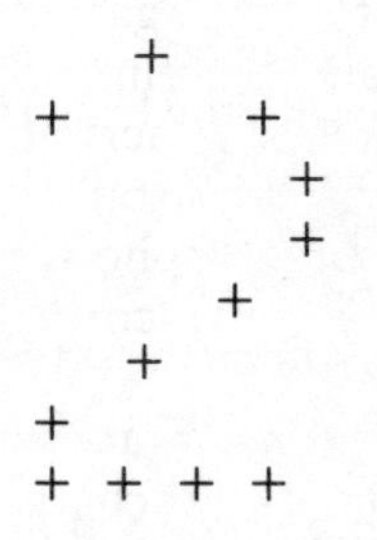

As they approached the airfield and tightened the formation, the middle two of the back four hit the jet-wash of the aircraft in front. Their wings overlapped until 2's wing tip hit 3's engine nacelle, turning off his main fuel cock and jamming 2's aileron. The result was that both quickly fell away from the formation so that just as it came overhead, much to the amusement of members of other squadrons watching on the ground, their proud figure 2 became a question mark!

The two damaged aircraft landed safely, but the atmosphere in the mess bars that evening was not quite what No 2 Squadron had had in mind.

Flight Lieutenant A. C. East

## Of Birds and Bees and Flying Machines

When I went up to university I had already decided to try and join the University Air Squadron. The first series of interviews went well and I was selected for the next stage, which was to be an interview with the CO and his chief instructor. I knew they were going to ask a question that would require some pre-thought from me if I was to get selected, sure enough it came up: 'So you want to fly, do you? How many hours have you got?' said the CO. 'None, sir,' I replied. 'Well, how many times have you been in an aircraft?' asked the chief instructor. 'Only once, sir, when I was six. It was an old Mosquito on the ground at Wroughton.' I replied. Immediately the CO jumped in, as it looked as though I was one candidate that he could easily dismiss: 'Well, boy, how do you know you would like flying?' I gave him my pre-thought answer: 'Sir, how did you know that you would like sex before you tried it?' He, amidst great roars of laughter, said, 'You're in!' and I was, and that was the start of my flying career.

Wing Commander M. W. Streten

# An After-dinner Tale . . .

I was a young Senior Aircraftsman (SAC) in Aden in 1966–7 and running a small combined mess at a unit called RAF Hiswa (Transmitter site) half way between Aden and little Aden. I was the senior SAC (by three months) and was in charge for the AOC's inspection.

Come the big day, I had my Arab staff all lined up to meet 'The Big Nebby', as the Arabs called him. They were all stood in a line neat and tidy in crisp new cooks' whites, all with the fold marks still in them, as opposed to their normal dress of singlet, trousers and flip-flops.

The AOC arrived. He was the late Sir Augustus Walker. I introduced him to the Arab staff, starting with the head chef, and so on down the line in the right pecking order. All the Arabs saluted him like guardsmen, i.e. their hands a few inches above their heads.

All went well until I introduced him to Ali Quassim (my cleaner). Picture if you can a nut-brown old man sixty-three years old, bald with a bit of grey and ginger frizz around the edges, a real character who hated Yemenis. He was totally loyal to the crown and his bosses. He had just purchased a new young wife for 3,000 shillings, a young thing, so he looked quite worn out. The conversation went like this:

AOC: 'Now who is this?'

ME: 'This is Ali Quassim, sir, my local national cleaner.'

AOC: 'Hello, Ali Quassim, how are you?'

Ali (Saluting like a Grenadier): 'Hello, Nebby, sir. Italian bastard shoot me up the arse in the war, but all is OK now, thank you, sir.'

AOC (Somehow with a straight face): 'I'm very glad to hear it, Ali Quassim.'

Turning to me, he congratulated me on the standard of the kitchen and staff, and left to a chorus of 'Goodbye, Nebby' from the Arabs, but as he was walking out of the kitchen, you could see his shoulders going up and down as he attempted to stifle his laughter.

Later in the day my CO, a flight lieutenant, came to the kitchen. I apologised for Ali Quassim's comments, to which he replied, 'Forget it, you have made his trip. He estimates it will be a long time before he has to write a speech for his dinner parties and mess functions, as you have given him the perfect after-dinner tale. Well done.'

Flight Sergeant H. Instone